Building a Solid Personal Finance Foundation in Your 20s

You're finished with school and entering the workforce. You want to make sure you create a firm foundation for your personal finances. Keep the following in mind when you start:

- ✔ **Get a checkup:** Just as you benefit from a health checkup, be sure to get a checkup on your finances to ensure that you're making the most of your money and your financial decisions.

- ✔ **Determine what you need with transaction and savings accounts and evaluate which banks and other financial firms offer accounts that best meet your needs.** Be on guard for high fees that erode your savings.

- ✔ **Celebrate the savings habit.** The earlier in life you're able to save money regularly, the smaller the portion of your income you'll need to save to accomplish a given goal. Scrutinize your current spending so that you know where your money is going and you can identify what to do about it.

- ✔ **Be on the lookout for spending reduction opportunities.** Regularly saving money, especially on a modest income, is challenging. I present many ideas for reducing your spending, but ultimately, how you cut your spending is a matter of personal preference.

- ✔ **Understand good and bad debt.** Debt can be a useful tool to enable the purchase of real estate or other valuable assets. Avoid consumer debt, such as on credit cards and auto loans. Consumer debt tends to be costly, and the interest isn't tax-deductible.

Grasping with Finances and Daily Living in Your 20s

Getting a paycheck and having a job requires more responsibility. Be sure to consider these important points when you're encountering finances in your 20s:

- ✔ **Know and manage your credit score.** Your *credit score* is a number which quantifies for lenders how likely you are to repay debts. Periodically access your credit reports, which you can do for free, and understand the steps you can take, as needed, to boost your credit score. Also take steps to protect your identity.

✔ **Consider all options before deciding to rent or buy.** Renting and sharing living space can be both economical and fun if you avoid the pitfalls. Buying and owning may make sense if you see yourself staying put for an extended period of time.

✔ **Communicate with your partner about money.** Money is often a source of friction in relationships. Thinking about money and planning how to manage it upfront with loved ones is usually time well spent.

Protecting Yourself and Your Income

Insurance plays a significant role in protecting your interests, including your health, your income, your property, and so on. Make sure you insure the following:

✔ **Your health:** Though you may feel that you're not likely to need it, having health insurance is wise. With a properly designed plan, you can contain the cost and get needed coverage.

✔ **Your income:** Even if you have no dependents, you depend on your income, so you should have long-term disability insurance. And if you have dependents, you may need life insurance, too.

✔ **Your possessions:** Insurance on your car, home, and other valuable possessions protects those assets from loss and protects you from lawsuits. Beware, though, of small-stuff policies that aren't worth buying.

Praise for Eric Tyson

"Eric Tyson is doing something important — namely, helping people at all income levels to take control of their financial futures. This book is a natural outgrowth of Tyson's vision that he has nurtured for years. Like Henry Ford, he wants to make something that was previously accessible only to the wealthy accessible to middle-income Americans."

> — James C. Collins, coauthor of the national bestseller *Built to Last;* former Lecturer in Business, Stanford Graduate School of Business

"*Personal Finance For Dummies* is the perfect book for people who feel guilty about inadequately managing their money but are intimidated by all of the publications out there. It's a painless way to learn how to take control."

> — National Public Radio's *Sound Money*

"Eric Tyson . . . seems the perfect writer for a *For Dummies* book. He doesn't tell you what to do or consider doing without explaining the why's and how's — and the booby traps to avoid — in plain English. . . . It will lead you through the thickets of your own finances as painlessly as I can imagine."

> — *Chicago Tribune*

"This book provides easy-to-understand personal financial information and advice for those without great wealth or knowledge in this area. Practitioners like Eric Tyson, who care about the well-being of middle-income people, are rare in today's society."

> — Joel Hyatt, founder of Hyatt Legal Services, one of the nation's largest general-practice personal legal service firms

More Bestselling For Dummies Titles by Eric Tyson

Investing For Dummies

A *Wall Street Journal* bestseller, this book walks you through how to build wealth in stocks, real estate, and small business as well as other investments.

Mutual Funds For Dummies

This best-selling guide is now updated to include current fund and portfolio recommendations. Using the practical tips and techniques, you'll design a mutual fund investment plan suited to your income, lifestyle, and risk preferences.

Taxes For Dummies

The complete, best-selling reference for completing your tax return and making tax-wise financial decisions year-round. Tyson coauthors this book with tax experts David Silverman and Margaret Munro.

Home Buying For Dummies

America's #1 real estate book includes coverage of online resources in addition to sound financial advice from Eric Tyson and frontline real estate insights from industry veteran Ray Brown. Also available from America's best-selling real estate team of Tyson and Brown — *House Selling For Dummies* and *Mortgages For Dummies.*

Real Estate Investing For Dummies

Real estate is a proven wealth-building investment, but many people don't know how to go about making and managing rental property investments. Real estate and property management expert Robert Griswold and Eric Tyson cover the gamut of property investment options, strategies, and techniques.

Personal Finance in Your 20s

FOR

DUMMIES®

by Eric Tyson, MBA

Author of *Personal Finance For Dummies* and

Personal Finance For Seniors For Dummies

WILEY

John Wiley & Sons, Inc.

Personal Finance in Your 20s For Dummies®

Published by
John Wiley & Sons, Inc.
111 River St.
Hoboken, NJ 07030-5774
www.wiley.com

Copyright © 2011 by Eric Tyson

Published by John Wiley & Sons, Inc., Hoboken, New Jersey

Published simultaneously in Canada

WILEY

About the Author

Eric Tyson is an internationally acclaimed and bestselling personal finance author and speaker who operates one of the Web's most popular personal finance sites at www.eric tyson.com. He has worked with and taught people from all financial situations, so he knows the financial concerns and questions of real folks. Despite having an MBA from the Stanford Graduate School of Business and a BS in economics and biology from Yale University, Eric remains a master of "keeping it simple."

He figured out how to pursue his dream after working as a management consultant to Fortune 500 financial-service firms. Eric took his inside knowledge of the banking, investment, and insurance industries and committed himself to making personal financial management accessible to all.

He is the author of five national bestselling financial books in Wiley Publishing's *For Dummies* series, including books on personal finance, investing, mutual funds, home buying (coauthor), and real estate investing (coauthor). His *Personal Finance For Dummies* won the Benjamin Franklin Award for best business book of the year. An accomplished personal finance writer, his "Investors' Guide" syndicated column, distributed by King Features, is read by millions nationally, and he was an award-winning columnist for the *San Francisco Examiner.*

Eric's work has been featured and quoted in hundreds of local and national publications, including *Newsweek, The Wall Street Journal, Los Angeles Times, Chicago Tribune, Forbes, Kiplinger's Personal Finance, Parenting, Money, Family Money,* and *Bottom Line/Personal;* on NBC's *Today Show,* ABC, CNBC, PBS's *Nightly Business Report,* CNN, and FOX; and on CBS national radio, NPR's *Marketplace Money,* Bloomberg Business Radio, and the Business Radio Network.

Eric's Web site is www.erictyson.com.

Dedication

This book is hereby and irrevocably dedicated to my family and friends, as well as to my counseling clients and customers, who ultimately have taught me everything that I know about how to explain financial terms and strategies so that all of us may benefit.

Author's Acknowledgments

I hold many people accountable for my perverse and maniacal interest in figuring out money matters and the financial-services industry, but most of the blame falls on my loving parents, Charles and Paulina, who taught me most of what I know that's been of use in the real world.

I'd also like to thank Rocky Shepard and all the good folks at King Features for believing in and supporting my writing and teaching.

Many thanks to all the people who provided insightful comments on this book, especially and including Ben Popken and Maria Bruno.

And thanks to all the wonderful people on the front line and behind the scenes at my publisher, Wiley Publishing, especially Erin Mooney, Mike Baker, and Chad Sievers.

Publisher's Acknowledgments

We're proud of this book; please send us your comments at http://dummies. custhelp.com. For other comments, please contact our Customer Care Department within the U.S. at 877-762-2974, outside the U.S. at 317-572-3993, or fax 317-572-4002.

Some of the people who helped bring this book to market include the following:

Acquisitions, Editorial, and Media Development

Senior Project Editor: Chad R. Sievers

Acquisitions Editor: Erin Calligan Mooney

Copy Editor: Todd Lothery

Assistant Editor: David Lutton

Technical Editors: Maria Bruno CFP, Vanguard Investment Strategy Group, and Ben Popken

Editorial Manager: Michelle Hacker

Editorial Assistant: Jennette ElNaggar

Art Coordinator: Alicia B. South

Cover Photos: ©iStockphoto.com / Amanda Rohde

Cartoons: Rich Tennant (www.the5thwave.com)

Composition Services

Project Coordinator: Patrick Redmond

Layout and Graphics: Carl Byers, Lavonne Roberts

Proofreaders: Lauren Mandelbaum, Bonnie Mikkelson

Indexer: Glassman Indexing Services

Publishing and Editorial for Consumer Dummies

Diane Graves Steele, Vice President and Publisher, Consumer Dummies

Kristin Ferguson-Wagstaffe, Product Development Director, Consumer Dummies

Ensley Eikenburg, Associate Publisher, Travel

Kelly Regan, Editorial Director, Travel

Publishing for Technology Dummies

Andy Cummings, Vice President and Publisher, Dummies Technology/ General User

Composition Services

Debbie Stailey, Director of Composition Services

Contents at a Glance

Contents

Introduction

∙∙

*Y*our late teens and 20s are such an exciting time. During this period you're experiencing some dramatic changes in your life, exploring new endeavors, making your way in the world, trying new things, and meeting new people.

But as with anything else in life, your teens and 20s can be a scary time as well. Maybe you've experienced a failed relationship and a broken heart. Maybe you have to deal with a difficult boss or a job you don't like — or perhaps you're in danger of losing your job.

And then there are the money issues. Most of you are out of the nest and out from under your parents' wings, and your 20s are when you experience firsthand earning your own money and paying your own expenses. This isn't true for all twenty-somethings, of course, because some folks still live at home or have some financial dependence on their folks — maybe that's why *they* bought you this book! No matter your living situation, your 20s can be a challenging time, but this friendly guide can help make your 20s a bit smoother.

About This Book

Based on my experiences teaching classes, counseling clients, writing articles and books, and corresponding with friends, family, and people through my Web site, I've discovered how important having healthy and strong personal finances is. With that in mind, I designed and wrote this book to help you begin to lay a strong financial foundation. Your 20s are the best time to start.

I've worked with and taught people from all financial situations, so I know the financial concerns and questions of real folks just like you. Believe it or not, I first became interested in money matters when, as a middle school student, my father was laid off and received some retirement money. I worked with my dad to make investing decisions with the money. A couple of years later, I won my high school's science fair with a project on what influences the stock market.

In my 20s, I worked hard to keep my living expenses low and save money so that I could leave my job and pursue my entrepreneurial ideas. I accomplished that goal in my late 20s. My goal in writing this book is to give you lots of tools and information to help you get your personal finances in order so you, too, can meet your goals and dreams.

I also wrote this book to protect you; to watch your back. Hucksters out to separate you from your hard-earned money know an easy mark when they see one and being young and, therefore, less experienced makes you a target. The information and advice in this book can help you identify and steer around common pitfalls and bad deals before you get hit.

Conventions Used in This Book

To help you navigate the waters of this book, I've set up a few conventions:

- ✓ I use *italics* for emphasis and to highlight new words or terms that I define.
- ✓ I use **boldface** text to indicate the action part of numbered steps and to highlight key words or phrases in bulleted lists.
- ✓ I put all Web sites in `monofont` for easy identification.

What You're Not to Read

I organized this book so you can find information easily and easily understand what you find. And although I'd like to believe that you want to pore over every last word between the two yellow-and-black covers, I actually make it easy for you to identify "skippable" material. *Sidebars* — the shaded boxes that appear here and there — include helpful information and observations but aren't necessary reading.

Foolish Assumptions

No matter what your current situation is — whether you're
entering the job market right after school, graduating college
with or without student loans, living with your parents, or
living on your own — I thought of you as I wrote this book. I
made some assumptions about you:

✔ You want expert advice about important financial topics —
    such as getting a financial checkup, budgeting, paying off
    some debt, boosting your credit score, or investing — and
    you want answers quickly.

✔ Or perhaps you want a crash course in personal finance
    and are looking for a book you can read cover to cover to
    help solidify major financial concepts and get you think-
    ing about your finances in a more comprehensive way.

✔ Or maybe you're just tired of feeling financially frazzled
    and want to get better organized and on top of your
    money matters.

This book is basic enough to help a novice get his or her arms
around thorny financial issues. But readers who are a bit
more advanced in financial matters will be challenged, as well,
to think about their finances in a new way and identify areas
for improvement.

How This Book Is Organized

This book is organized into six parts, with each covering a
major area of your personal finances. The chapters within
each part cover specific topics in detail. Here's a summary of
what you can find in each part.

Part 1: Building Your Foundation

In this part, I start with the basics. First, I help you conduct a
financial checkup. My checkups help you answer important
questions. In this part, I also discuss getting the right bank
account for your situation, budgeting, strategizing about how
to spend less and save more, and paying down debts and
loans. Get these things right, and you're well on your way to a
healthy financial present and future!

Part II: Grown-up Stuff

After you're out and about in the real world, you have to deal with a host of new issues. You have your credit reports and credit score, which can impact your ability to borrow money and the interest rate you're charged. You should take steps to protect against identity theft, for which you're at a greater risk. You'll be making housing commitments, most likely through a rental and possibly with roommates. And you may be saving money to buy a place to call your own. If you fall in love and merge your finances with another, though you may have opportunities for personal growth, you could get burned, too. I address all these topics and more in this part.

Part III: Earning More (And Keeping More of What You Earn)

If you're like most young people, your biggest asset is likely your future income-earning potential. That's why the first chapter in this part deals with making the most of your career. As you earn money, whether from employment or investments, you'll get hit with taxes, so I also address how to intelligently and legally reduce your tax bill. Last but not least, I explain how to make wise investments and construct and manage a portfolio in the years ahead.

Part IV: Insurance: You're Not as Invincible or Independent as You Think!

When you're young, you generally enjoy good health and don't have many financial obligations and commitments, so you don't need as much insurance, either in type or amount, as a middle-aged person with a family does. That said, you probably need more insurance than you may realize. Everyone needs health insurance, and if you're working, you should have disability coverage as well if you depend on your own income. If you drive a car, you need proper auto insurance, and you should have some coverage on where you live, too. This part details what insurance policies and features you need and how to get the best deal on each.

Part V: Your Information Diet

You're awash in information and advice. Most of it revolves around selling you something, especially through advertising, which increasingly is merged with content and advice. In this important part, I discuss various information sources and expose the truth and warts of each. Hiring some professional help may make sense for you, so I also explain what to look for (and look out for) in the folks you may employ.

Part VI: The Part of Tens

In this fun part, I present some lists of ten-somethings that can help you with your finances. Among the topics covered in this part are ten ways to save on car expenses and ten things more important than money.

Icons Used in This Book

The icons in this book help you find information you need:

This target flags strategy recommendations for making the most of your money.

This icon points out information that you definitely want to remember.

This icon marks things to avoid and points out common mistakes people make when managing their finances.

This icon alerts you to scams and scoundrels who prey on the unsuspecting.

This icon tells you when you should consider doing some additional research. Don't worry — I explain what to look for and what to look out for.

Where to Go from Here

This book is organized so you can go wherever you want to find complete information. Want advice on maximizing your credit score, for example? Go to Part II for that. You can use the table of contents to find broad categories of information or the index to look up more specific topics.

If you're not sure where to go, you may want to start with Part I. It gives you all the basic info you need to assess your financial situation and points to places where you can find more detailed information for improving it.

Part I

Building Your Foundation

In this part . . .

1 discuss the basics of sound personal financial management, beginning with a checkup to help you diagnose
your current situation. You find out ways to make the
most of bank and other transaction accounts, tips on budgeting and saving, strategies for reducing your spending,
and details on paying back loans and debts.

Chapter 1

Your Financial Checkup

*H*ow's your health? I don't mean your financial health; I mean your personal, physical health. Are you active and getting exercise several times per week? Is your weight appropriate for your height? How's your blood pressure? What's your energy level like, and how much sleep are you getting nightly? What are your cholesterol, HDL, and LDL levels?

Most people in their 20s don't have to worry about these types of questions. But whether you've had health issues or not, do you know the answers? Some people do but many people don't, especially if they haven't visited a doctor in quite some time or think of themselves as otherwise healthy.

In my experience, the same is true with personal finances. You probably know the name of the last restaurant you ate at and the most recent movie you saw, but you probably don't know your money vital signs. In this chapter, I'm your financial doc, and I'm here to help you evaluate your net worth, savings rate, credit health, investment portfolio, and insurance coverage.

Calculating Your Worth

Having a sense of what you own (your *assets*) and what you owe (your *liabilities*) is important because it provides some measure of your financial security and your ability to accomplish financial goals such as buying a home, starting a business, or retiring someday.

In this section, I define net worth and then walk you through the relatively simple calculations of determining your own personal net worth.

Defining net worth

Your *net worth* is quite simply your *financial assets* (for example, bank and investment accounts) minus your *financial liabilities* (debts such as student loans and credit card debt). In the following sections, I walk you through how to perform these calculations.

When I discuss your monetary *net worth,* I'm not talking about personal possessions. Your car, stereo system, television, computer, and other personal items all have some value, of course. If you need to sell them, you could get something for them on eBay. But the reality is that you're unlikely to accumulate personal items with the purpose of later selling them to finance such personal goals as buying a home, starting a business, retiring, and so forth. After all, these things are investments and decline rapidly in value after purchase.

Figuring what you own: Financial assets

To calculate your financial assets, get out your bank statements and investment account statements, including retirement accounts and any other paperwork that can help you. You may have only one or two accounts, and that's fine. Add up all the values of these accounts to find out what you own.

It's perfectly normal for most folks under 30 to be just starting out in terms of accumulating assets. This book is going to help you change and improve upon that.

Valuing Social Security and pensions

Now or in the years ahead, you may accumulate some retirement benefits based on your years of work. You may do so through the federal government's Social Security program and/or through an employer's pension plan.

When you work and earn money, your employer (or you if you're self-employed) pays taxes into Social Security, which earns you future Social Security retirement income benefits. Under current laws, which of course may change, you're eligible to receive full Social Security benefits at age 67. (You may collect a benefit reduced by 30 percent if you begin receiving your Social Security payments at age 62.)

In surveys, most young people say that they're more likely to believe in things like UFOs than in actually getting money out of Social Security! Although being skeptical and questioning things is useful, I say that such deep cynicism about Social Security isn't well founded. Those who are eligible to receive benefits (which are generally folks who've paid Social Security taxes above relatively low threshold amounts over at least ten years in total) should get them.

Some employers provide a retirement benefit known as a *pension* that's paid to you in retirement based on your years of service (employment) with the organization. Your employer puts aside money over and above your salary compensation into a separate account to fund your future pension payments. Pension plans are more common in public sector organizations (governments, schools, and so on) and larger companies, especially those with labor unions. Pension plans are generally insured/guaranteed by government agency entities.

In addition to excluding personal property and possessions because folks don't generally sell those to accomplish their personal and financial goals, I would also probably exclude your home as an asset if you happen to own one. You can include it if you expect to downsize or to rent in retirement and live off of some of your home's equity.

Now, I do have one exception to something that isn't generally thought of as a financial asset, which you may or may not want to include in this category. Some people have valuable collections of particular items, be they coins, baseball cards, or whatever. You can count such collections as assets, but remember that they're only real assets if you'd be willing to sell them and use the proceeds toward one of your goals.

Determining what you owe: Financial liabilities

Most people accumulate debts and loans during periods in life when their expenditures exceed their income. I did that when I went through college. You may have student loans, an auto loan, and credit card debts. Get out any statements that document your loans and debts and figure out the total of them all.

Netting the difference

After you total your financial assets and your financial liabilities, you can subtract the latter from the former to arrive at your *net worth*.

Most folks in their 20s have a very small or negative net worth. There's no point wringing your hands over the results — you can't change history. But you can change the direction of your finances in the future and boost your net worth surprisingly fast. First, you have to figure your savings rate and how to increase it, which is the topic I discuss next.

Grasping the Importance of Savings

To accomplish important personal and financial goals such as buying a home, starting a business, traveling, and retiring someday, most folks need to save money. Some exceptions do exist, such as those fortunate people who have trust funds or inherit significant enough sums that they don't need to save money from their work earnings. But the vast majority of people must save in order to accomplish their goals.

You can't effectively save up for a long-term goal if you don't know what your savings rate is. When I worked as a financial counselor and taught adult education money-management courses, I was struck by how few people knew the rate at which they were saving money. Most people can tell you what they earned from their work over the past year, but few folks really know what portion of their employment income they were able to save. That's because to have an accurate idea of this percentage, you really need to do some analysis and calculations. The math isn't that complicated, but it does require some time and effort, especially if you haven't been tracking your spending or net worth over the past year. In the following sections, I explain a couple of different ways to calculate your savings rate over the past year.

Netting your income and spending

The first way to determine your savings rate is to tally your employment income and expenses over the past year. By subtracting your total expenses, including taxes, from the past year from your employment income, you can arrive at *net savings.*

The *employment income* part of the equation is simple for most folks — it's simply the total amount of your paychecks from work. But unless you systematically track your spending, that piece of the puzzle is a lot more work to figure. I walk you through how to compile your spending in Chapter 3.

Assessing the change in your net worth

If you don't want to be bothered with the time-consuming task of tabulating your spending over the past year, here's an alternative method for arriving at your savings rate that may be quicker for you. Follow these few easy steps, and fill in the blanks in Table 1-1.

1. **Calculate your net worth.**

   Refer to the earlier section "Netting the difference" for an explanation of how to do so.

2. **Calculate your net worth from one year ago.**

   You can determine your year-ago net worth by tallying your financial assets (savings and investments) from one year ago and subtracting your financial liabilities (loans and debts) from one year ago. Don't count your home as an asset or your mortgage as a liability. Your concern here is financial assets.

3. Correct for any changes in value of investments you owned the past year.

Suppose that your net worth today is $15,000, whereas one year ago it was $10,000. You might conclude from the change in your net worth that you've saved $5,000 ($15,000 – $10,000), but that figure may not be correct and here's why. A year ago when you had a net worth of $10,000, you presumably had savings and investments, and those would have changed in value over the past year. Suppose you made some good investments and they produced $1,000 in returns (from interest, dividends, appreciation, and so on) over the past 12 months. Though you're happy to have made $1,000 on your investments, that money isn't new savings and shouldn't be counted in your savings rate calculations. So you really saved $4,000 ($5,000 – $1,000).

Conversely, if your net worth was reduced over the past year by declines in the value of your investments, you should add back that figure when determining your savings rate. If your investments declined by $1,500 in value over the past year, you really saved $6,500 ($5,000 + $1,500). Table 1-1 walks you through this part of the analysis.

If you have debt that you've been paying down over the past year, you can count the principal payment reduction on that debt as savings. For example, suppose a year ago you owed $5,000 on an auto loan. Now, a year later, you owe just $4,500. You can count that $500 reduction in what you owe as new savings.

Table 1-1   Your Savings Rate over the Past Year

Calculate your net worth now and one year ago	
Today	*One Year Ago*
Savings & investments $_____	Savings & investments $_____
= Net worth today $_____	= Net worth a year ago $_____

Correct for changes in value of investments you owned the past year	
Net worth today	$_____
− Net worth a year ago	$_____
− Appreciation of investments (over past year)	$_____
+ Depreciation of investments (over past year)	$_____
= Savings amount	$_____
Savings rate	_____
Annual employment income	$_____

Understanding and Improving Your Credit Score

If you expect to someday apply for a loan of any type and want to pay a low rate of interest, you should understand your credit report and credit score and how to improve them. A *credit report* is basically your credit history, while a *credit score* is a three-digit score based on the information in your personal credit report. This section highlights what you need to know about your credit score and reports, including how to obtain and improve them. Chapter 6 provides more insight into managing your credit report and credit score.

Deciphering how lenders use credit reports and scores

Most people borrow money at various times in their life, whether it's to buy a home or other real estate, to finance a small business, or for other purposes. When you want to borrow money, lenders examine your credit report and your credit score(s) to determine how responsible you've been with credit and to help them decide whether they should lend you money (and if so, how much to charge you).

Specifically, lenders examine your history of credit usage in your credit report. This information tells the lender when each of your accounts was opened, what the recent balance is, whether you've made payments on time, and whether you've defaulted on any loans. A credit report also tells a prospective lender who has recently accessed your credit report and thus would indicate where else you've been applying for credit.

Lenders use your credit score to help them predict the likelihood that you'll default on repaying your borrowings. The higher your credit score the better, because a high credit score means that you have a lower likelihood of defaulting on a loan. Thus, more lenders will be willing to extend you credit and charge you lower rates for that credit.

The most widely used credit score is the FICO score, which was developed by Fair, Isaac and Company. FICO scores range from a low of 300 to a high of 850. Most scores fall in the 600s and 700s, and the median is around 720. You generally qualify for the best lending rates if your credit score is in the mid-700s or higher.

Obtaining your credit reports and fixing errors

You want to get your hands on your credit report so you know what lenders are reviewing. You're entitled to receive a free copy of your credit report (which does *not* contain your credit score) every 12 months from each of the three credit bureaus — Equifax, Experian, and TransUnion. If you visit www.annualcreditreport.com, you can view and print copies of your credit report from each of the three credit agencies. Alternatively, you can call 877-322-8228 and request that your reports be mailed to you.

When you receive your reports, inspect them for possible mistakes. Credit reporting bureaus and the creditors who report credit information to these bureaus make plenty of errors.

If your problems are fixable, you can fix them yourself, but you have to make some phone calls or write a letter or two. Some credit report errors arise from other people's negative information getting on your credit report. This can happen if you have a common name, have moved a lot, or for other reasons. If the problematic information on your report appears not to be yours, tell that particular credit bureau and explain that you need more information because you don't recognize the creditor.

Creditors are the source of some reporting mistakes as well. If that's the case with your report, write or call the creditor to get the incorrect information fixed. Phoning first usually works best. (The credit bureau should be able to tell you how to reach the creditor if you don't know how.) If necessary, follow up with a letter. You can also dispute errors online directly from your credit report.

Whether you speak with a credit bureau or an actual lender, make notes of your conversations. If representatives say that they can fix the problem, get their name and extension, and follow up with them if they don't deliver the promised results. If you're ensnared in bureaucratic red tape, escalate the situation by speaking with a department manager. By law, bureaus are required to respond to a request to fix a credit error within 30 days. And if you file a dispute and the creditor doesn't respond, the derogatory item gets removed.

You and a creditor may not see eye to eye on a problem, and the creditor may refuse to budge. If that's the case, credit bureaus are required by law to allow you to add a 100-word explanation to your credit file. Just remember that if you go this route, be factual in your write-up and steer clear of broad attacks on the creditor (such as "their customer service sucks").

Avoid "credit repair" firms that claim to be able to fix your credit report problems. In the worst cases I've seen, these firms charge outrageous amounts of money and don't come close to fulfilling their marketing hype. If you have legitimate glitches on your credit report, credit repair firms can't make the glitches disappear. You can fix errors on your own without the charge.

Getting your credit score

Many folks are disappointed to find that their credit reports lack their credit score. The reason for this is quite simple: The 2003 law mandating that the three credit agencies provide a free credit report annually to each U.S. citizen who requests a copy did *not* mandate that they provide the credit score. Thus, if you want to obtain your credit score, it's generally going to cost you.

One circumstance allows you to get one of your credit scores for free, but unfortunately, you can only do so when you're turned down for a loan. The 2010 financial reform bill allows you to obtain a free copy of the credit score a lender used in making a negative decision regarding your desired loan.

 Otherwise, you can request your credit score from Fair, Isaac and Company for $15.95 for each request. Alternatively, I recommend calling a credit bureau's toll-free phone number to buy your credit score rather than visiting the credit bureau's Web site, because finding the proper Web page to buy your credit score on a one-time basis without getting signed up for other, ongoing, far more costly services and monitoring is a nightmare.

 Consider buying your FICO credit score if you're in the market for a loan and have some reason to be concerned that your credit score isn't stellar. Alternatively, for no out-of-pocket cost, you can try the FICO score simulator at `www.myfico.com/ficocreditscoreestimator/`, which provides an estimate of your FICO score based on your answers to a series of questions about your credit usage and credit history.

 If you do spring for your current credit score or use the credit score estimator, be clear about what you're buying or getting. You may not realize that you're agreeing to some sort of ongoing credit monitoring service for, say, $50 to $100+ per year. I don't recommend spending money on those services. Instead, for free, request your credit report from one of the three agencies every four months.

 A number of Web-based entities such as Credit Karma and Quizzle claim to provide you with your credit score for "free." These sites don't give you the FICO credit score that lenders most often use. Instead, the sites, which do a poor job of disclosure, give you one of the credit scores developed by the credit reporting bureaus, such as the TransUnion VantageScore.

In addition to getting a largely useless credit score at such sites, remember that you're sharing with them an enormous amount of confidential information about yourself. How some of these sites make money isn't completely clear, but I can guarantee you that it involves finding ways (legal, hopefully) of tapping into all that information you give them. For example, a larger company that's heavily involved in mortgage lending and other real estate activities owns Quizzle, so you can guess why Quizzle would like to get their tentacles into consumers who are investigating their credit scores.

Improving your credit reports and score

Take an interest in improving your credit standing and score rather than throwing money away to buy your credit score or paying for some ongoing monitoring service to which you may not pay attention. Working to boost your credit rating is especially worthwhile if you know that your credit report contains detrimental information or if your score is lower than 750.

Here are the most important actions that you can take to boost your attractiveness to lenders:

- ✔ **Check your credit reports for accuracy.** Correct any errors, and be especially sure to get accounts removed if they aren't yours and they show late payments or are in collection. Refer to the earlier section "Obtaining your credit reports and fixing errors" for more information.

- ✔ **Pay all your bills on time.** To ensure on-time payments, sign up for automatic bill payment, which most companies enable you to use.

- ✔ **Be loyal if it doesn't cost you.** The older the age of loan accounts you have open, the better for your credit rating. Closing old accounts and opening a bunch of new ones generally lowers your credit score, so don't jump at a new credit card offer unless it's really going to save you money (such as if you're carrying credit card debt at a high interest rate and want to transfer that balance to a lower-rate card). Ask your current credit card provider to match a lower rate you find elsewhere.

✓ **Limit your total debt and number of debt accounts.** The more loans, especially consumer loans, that you hold and the higher the balances, the lower your credit score will be. Work to pay down consumer revolving debt, such as on an auto loan and credit cards. See Chapter 5 for more information.

Comprehending Your Investment Options

If you're like most folks under the age of 30, you probably don't have much (or even any) money invested. That's fine for now, because together, we're going to address that in this book. Regardless of how much (or how little) you have invested in banks, mutual funds, or other types of accounts, you want to invest your money in the wisest way possible and have it grow over time without exposing it to extraordinary risks.

In this section, I provide some background to help you understand how to best focus your efforts to become a more knowledgeable and successful investor. (In Part III, I delve into all the important details of investing.)

✓ **Investment options:** Making the best investments without understanding your range of options and the strengths and weaknesses of each is difficult. Do you understand the investments that you currently own, including their potential returns and risks? If you invest in or plan to invest in individual stocks, do you understand how to evaluate a stock, including reviewing the company's balance sheet, income statement, competitive position, price-earnings ratio versus its peer group, and so on?

Last but not least are issues that come up if you work with a financial advisor for investment advice. Do you understand what that person is recommending that you do, are you comfortable with those actions and that advisor, and is that person compensated in a way that minimizes potential conflicts of interest in the strategies and investments he or she recommends? Flip to Chapter 17 for advice on hiring professionals.

✔ **Tax considerations:** For most working people, taxes are either the number one or two largest expense categories. For starters, do you know what marginal income tax bracket (combined federal and state) you're in, and do you factor that in when selecting investments? For money outside of retirement accounts, do you understand how these investments produce income and gains and whether these types of investments make the most sense from the standpoint of your tax situation?

✔ **Short-term money:** *Short-term money* includes money you'd use in an emergency or for a major purchase within the next few years. Do you have enough money set aside for short-term emergencies and is that money in an investment where the principal doesn't fluctuate in value? Is the money that you're going to need for a major expenditure in the next few years invested in a conservative, low-volatility investment?

✔ **Long-term money:** *Long-term money* includes money set aside for longer-term use such as for retirement. Do you have your money in different, diversified investments that aren't dependent on one or a few securities or one type of investment (that is, bonds, stocks, real estate, and so on)? Is the money that you've earmarked for longer-term purposes (more than five years) invested to produce returns that are likely to stay ahead of inflation?

Examining Insurance Coverage

Just about everyone despises spending money on insurance. Who enjoys thinking about risks and possible catastrophes and then shopping for insurance to protect against those risks? Therein lies some major reasons why most people don't have all the coverage they really need and don't get the best value when they do buy insurance. But folks who've suffered a major loss understand the security provided by a good policy.

In Part IV, I discuss everything you need to know about insurance, including what policies you do and don't need. Here are the major points to consider as you review your insurance knowledge:

✔ **Smart shopping:** Do you know when it makes sense to buy insurance through discount brokers, fee-for-service advisors, and companies that sell directly to the public (bypassing agents) — and when it doesn't? Do you shop around for the best price on your insurance policies at least every couple of years? Do you know whether your insurance companies have good track records when it comes to paying claims and keeping customers satisfied?

✔ **Coverage understanding:** Do you understand the individual coverages, protection types, and amounts of each insurance policy you have? Does your current insurance protection make sense given your current personal and financial situation (as opposed to your situation when you bought the policies)?

✔ **Income protection:** If you wouldn't be able to make it financially without your employment income, do you have adequate long-term disability insurance coverage? If you have family members who are dependent on your continued working income, do you have adequate life insurance coverage to replace your income should you die?

✔ **Liability protection:** Do you carry enough liability insurance on your home, car (including umbrella/excess liability), and business to protect all your assets?

Identifying Common Financial Mistakes

Your financial physical is complete if you've been working along with me since the beginning of this chapter. The results should help you best understand where you can get the biggest return on your time invested elsewhere in the book.

One motivation for reading the rest of the book is to reduce your chances of making common mistakes. Your 20s are a decade where lack of financial knowledge is exposed and reflected in the beginning of costly money mistakes such as

✔ **Spending excessively and accumulating consumer debt:** Too many young adults leave home being experts in spending without having learned much about living within their means and saving and investing. Many things may tempt you — the never-ending stream of gadgets and electronics, cars, restaurants, bars, nightclubs, new clothing, concerts, sporting events, and so on. Check out Chapter 4 for information about reducing your spending on items you don't need.

✔ **Defaulting on student loans or other debts:** This problem is often the consequence of the preceding problem of spending too much and accumulating too much debt. Being overwhelmed with debt, which may be exacerbated by a job loss or unexpected expenses, can cause folks to fall behind on their student loan or other debt payments. See Chapter 5 for information on paying down debts.

✔ **Experiencing failed relationships that damage your credit rating and financial health:** You know what they say about love being blind sometimes, right? Well, one of the things many twenty-somethings don't think about when in a relationship is how the things they're doing are going to work out or not work out should the relationship fail. Sharing bank accounts and bill paying may not present glaring problems when everything is going well, but you can quickly end up with a tarnished credit report should your love boat run aground. See Chapter 8 for info about relationships and money.

✔ **Falling behind on tax payments and violating tax laws:** Filing your annual tax return and making quarterly tax payments if you're self-employed aren't enjoyable tasks. In fact, you may find these chores downright intimidating and stressful. But if you fail to complete them correctly, or complete them at all, you could get socked with hefty interest and penalty charges and possibly do some jail time in the worst cases. Check out Chapter 10 for a complete discussion of paying taxes.

✔ **Making poor investments:** You work hard to earn money and then to save it. So you should do your homework to ensure that you invest it well. Don't rush into making an investment you don't understand because you have a lot to lose. There are plenty of slick-talking salesmen who will sell you an investment that helps to line their pockets but not yours. You also don't want your money sitting around for years on end in a low interest bank account, which is what happens to folks who don't know how to invest their money. Go to Chapter 11 for more in-depth information about investing your money.

✔ **Neglecting to secure proper insurance coverage:** Most young people don't spend a lot of time thinking about risks. After all, most teenagers and twenty-somethings are healthy and energetic. So things like health insurance or disability insurance seem unnecessary and for older folks. The good news is that insurance costs less when you're younger because you're less likely to suffer a major illness or disability than someone decades older than you. The chapters in Part IV detail more insurance stuff.

✔ **Being taken and duped by biased and/or shoddy advice:** Many companies and people have something to sell. Some of what they're selling is good stuff, much is mediocre, and some is downright awful. You don't need to pay high commissions or end up in the wrong type of investments or insurance. Check out Chapter 17 for what you need to know about dealing with professionals.

Chapter 2

Making the Best Use of Bank Accounts

*W*hile you were in school, you may have already had a savings or checking account to help you save money and pay some bills. Now that you're in the real world and out of school, you have to consider whether you want to make a longer-term commitment with a financial institution, such as a bank.

In this chapter, I walk you through your bank account choices and what investigative work you need to do to find the right bank for you. I also address some alternatives to having a bank account in the first place.

Identifying Your Options

When figuring out where to protect your hard-earned money, you have several choices. You want to select an institution that offers the services you need on attractive terms. The following sections outline these choices and provide some helpful information.

Brick-and-mortar banks

The most obvious choice for banking is using a local bank you pass by on a regular basis. Although these types of banks are conveniently located, these banks may not be the most cost efficient. You can find two main types of brick-and-mortar banks:

- **Small-town bank:** These banks only have a couple branches. Everyone knows your name. Hours are generally limited and you may face extra ATM fees for using ATMs that aren't at one of the bank's branches.

    A sometimes attractive, "small-town" banking option is credit unions. To join, you generally need to work for a particular employer (such as General Electric) or industry/occupation (for example, teachers). Thanks to a federal government exemption on income taxes, credit unions tend to be able to pay higher interest rates on deposits and charge lower rates on loans. Don't assume, however, that a local credit union always has the best deals; be sure to comparison shop. To locate credit unions near you, visit the Credit Union National Association Web site at www.creditunion.coop and click on the "Locate a Credit Union" link or call them at 800-358-5710.

- **Large chain bank:** Such banks tend to be regional, national, and sometimes even multinational. You may recognize their name from extensive advertising campaigns. They tend to have extensive ATM networks, which may reduce your ATM fees but you pay for it in other ways, such as through less-competitive terms (interest rate paid, service fees levied) on checking and savings accounts.

Later in this chapter, in the "Banking Online" section, I identify some universal questions you can ask when searching for a bank, no matter which kind of bank you use. If you want to use a brick-and-mortar bank, you may want to investigate these additional points:

Be sure to comparison shop among several banks and scrutinize their fees and interest rates on their checking accounts and any other type of account you may be interested in. Also, read the "Understanding Your Banking Account Options"

section later in this chapter, and read the rest of the chapter so that you're aware of your nonbank and Internet banking options.

Online banks

Although traditional banks with walk-in branch locations are shrinking in number because of closures and failures, online banking is growing — and for good reason. One of the biggest expenses of operating a traditional retail bank is the cost of the real estate and the related costs of the branch. Online banks generally don't have any or many retail branches and conduct their business mostly over the Internet and through the mail. By lowering its costs of doing business, the best online banks may offer better account terms, such as paying you higher interest rates on your account balances. Online banks can also offer better terms on loans.

Online banking is convenient, too — you can conduct most transactions more quickly on the Internet, and by banking online, you save the bank money, which enables the bank to offer you better account terms. And because online banking is generally available 24/7, you don't need to rush out at lunchtime to make it to your bank during its limited open hours.

Other choices

You can also place your money in a brokerage account or money market fund. If you want to consider other options that offer more attractive investment accounts and options, check out the later section "Considering Alternatives to Bank Accounts."

Understanding Your Banking Account Options

No matter what type of bank you choose, make sure that you have a firm grasp of the different account options. Doing so requires thinking about your banking needs and what's important to you and what's not. The following sections identify how you can protect your moolah with different accounts and access your money when you need it.

Transaction accounts

Whether it's paying monthly bills or having something in your wallet to make purchases with at retail stores, everyone needs the ability to conduct transactions. Two of the most common types of transaction accounts are as follows:

- ✔ **Checking accounts:** The most fundamental of bank accounts, a *checking account* enables you to pay bills (by check or electronic payments) and deposit money from your job (including through direct deposit). Interest paid is generally low or nonexistent, and you need to watch out for various fees.

During periods of low interest rates, the fees levied on a transaction account, such as a checking account, should be of greater concern to you than the interest paid on account balances. After all, you shouldn't be keeping lots of extra cash in a checking account; you have better options for that. I discuss those options later in this chapter.

Debit cards are excellent transaction cards. They connect to your checking account, thus eliminating the need for you to carry around excess cash. They carry a Visa or MasterCard logo and are widely accepted by merchants for purchases and for obtaining cash back from your checking account. And like a credit card, you can dispute transactions if the product or service you purchase with your debit card isn't what the seller claimed it would be and the seller fails to stand behind it. But unlike a credit card, debit cards have no credit feature, so you can't spend money that you don't have.

Because of new bank regulations, effective July 1, 2010, bank customers must now give their permission/consent in advance for overdraft protection and the associated fee from a debit card transaction. (Check and electronic bill payments still go through as they have in the past and can lead to an account being overdrawn.)

However, you can rack up overdraft fees if your bank processes debit card transactions that lead to your account being overdrawn.

✔ **Credit cards:** These transaction cards, which are offered by banks with either the Visa or MasterCard logo, enable you to make purchases and pay for them over time if you so choose.

I'm not a fan of credit cards because the credit feature enables you to spend money you don't have and carry a debt balance month to month. Notwithstanding the lower short-term interest rates some cards charge to lure new customers, the reality is that borrowing on credit cards is expensive — usually to the tune of about 17 percent. The smart way to use such a card is to pay the bill in full each month and avoid these high interest charges.

Options for getting cash

You need a firm understanding of the different features of the transaction accounts your bank offers so you can easily access your cash. You may think choosing a bank that has a large ATM network is your best option, but think again.

One reason that bank customers have gotten lousy terms on their accounts is that they gravitate toward larger banks and their extensive ATM networks so they can easily get cash when they need it. These ATM networks (and the often-associated bank branches) are costly for banks to maintain. So, you pay higher fees and get lower yields when you're the customer of a bank with a large ATM network — especially a bank that does tons of advertising.

Do you really need to carry a lot of cash and have access to a large ATM network? Probably not. A debit card is likely the better option for most people.

Savings accounts

Savings accounts are accounts for holding spare cash in order to earn some interest. Banks and credit unions generally pay higher interest rates on savings account balances than they do on checking account balances. But savings account interest rates have often lagged behind the rates of the best money market funds offered by mutual fund companies and brokerage firms. Online banking is changing that dynamic, however, and now the best banks and credit unions offer competitive rates on savings accounts.

The virtue of most savings accounts is that you can earn some interest yet have penalty-free access to your money. The investment doesn't fluctuate in value the way that a bond does, and you don't have early-withdrawal penalties as you do with a certificate of deposit (CD).

Banking Online

No matter if you choose a brick-and-mortar bank or strictly an online bank, technology has allowed people to do more and more of their banking on the Internet. With this benefit come some important points to remember to protect yourself and your dinero. In this section, I explain the best ways to evaluate an online bank and how to make the most of banking online.

Evaluating a bank: What to look for

When looking for a bank that fits your needs, put on your detective hat and get ready to search for the best deals. You don't want to pick a bank just because that's where your parents or co-worker banked.

So what do you look for? You first want to look for a bank that participates in the U.S. government–operated Federal Deposit Insurance Corporation (FDIC) program. Otherwise, if the bank fails, your money isn't protected. The FDIC covers your deposits at each bank up to a cool quarter million dollars.

Some online banks are able to offer higher interest rates because they're based overseas and, therefore, don't participate in the FDIC program. (Banks must pay insurance premiums into the FDIC fund, which, of course, adds to a bank's costs.) Another risk for you is noncovered banks that take excessive risks with their business to be able to pay depositors higher interest rates.

When considering doing business with an online bank or a smaller bank you haven't heard of, you should be especially careful to ensure that the bank is covered under the FDIC. And don't simply accept the bank's word for it or the bank's display of the FDIC logo in its offices or on its Web site.

Check the FDIC's Web site database of FDIC-insured institutions to see whether the bank you're considering doing business with is covered. Search by going to the FDIC's "Bank Find" page (`www2.fdic.gov/idasp/main_bankfind.asp`). You can search by bank name, city, state, or zip code of the bank. For insured banks, you can see the date it became insured, its insurance certificate number, the main office location for the bank (and branches), its primary government regulator, and other links to detailed information about the bank. In the event that your bank doesn't appear on the FDIC list yet the bank claims FDIC coverage, contact the FDIC at 877-275-3342.

In addition to ensuring that a bank is covered by the FDIC, also seek answers to these questions:

- ✔ **What's the bank's reputation for its services?** This may not be easy to discern, but at a minimum, you should conduct an Internet search of the bank's name along with the word "complaints" or "problems" and examine the results.

- ✔ **How accessible and knowledgeable are customer service people at the bank?** You want to be able to talk to a live, helpful person when you need help. Look for a phone number on the bank's Web site and call it to see how difficult reaching a live person is. Ask the customer service representatives questions to determine how knowledgeable and service oriented they are.

- ✔ **What's the process and options for withdrawing your money?** This issue is important to discuss with the bank's customer service people because you want convenient, low-cost access to your money. For example, if a bank lacks ATMs, what do they charge you for using other ATMs?

- ✔ **What are the fees for particular services?** You can probably find this information on the bank's Web site in a section called "accounts terms" or "disclosures." Also, look for the *Truth in Savings Disclosure,* which answers relevant account questions in a standardized format. Figure 2-1 shows an example of a bank's disclosure for its savings account.

TRUTH IN SAVINGS DISCLOSURE

Initial Deposit Requirement: There is no minimum deposit required to open the account.

Minimum Balance to Obtain Annual Percentage Yield (APY): There is no minimum balance required to obtain the disclosed APY.

Rate Information: The interest rate on your account is **1.09%** with an APY of **1.10%**. Your interest rate and APY may change. At our discretion we may change the interest rate for your account at any time.

Compounding and Crediting: Interest on your account is compounded and credited on a monthly basis.

Balance Computation Method: We use the daily balance method to calculate the interest on your account. This method applies a daily periodic rate to the principal in the account each day.

Accrual of Interest on Noncash Deposits: For all types of noncash deposits, interest begins to accrue not later than the second business day following the banking day on which the funds are deposited.

Fees: If we agree to process a wire transfer for you, the cost per transaction will be up to $40.00.

Transaction Limitations: You may transfer funds out of your savings account only to other accounts you have with us or to your linked account up to six times per monthly statement cycle using and combination of preauthorized, telephone, and automatic transfer services. If you exceed this limit on more than an occasional basis, we will close your account or transfer your funds to a transactional account. You are not limited in the number of transfers that you may make out of your account to repay loans at our bank. Wire transfers, if we agree to process them for you, are limited to $25,000 per day. We may also limit the number of wire transfers you can send each day.

Effect of Closing an Account: If you close your account before interest is credited, you will receive the accrued interest.

Figure 2-1: A bank's Truth in Savings Disclosure.

Protecting yourself online

The attractions of banking online are pretty obvious. For starters, banking on your computer whenever you want can be enormously convenient. You don't have to race around during your lunch break to find a local bank branch. And thanks to their lower overhead, the best online banks are able to offer competitive interest rates and account terms to their customers. Even if you go with a brick-and-mortar bank, you can usually also bank online.

You probably know from experience that conducting any type of transaction online is safe as long as you use some common sense and know who you're doing business with before you go forward. That said, others who've gone before you have gotten ripped off, so you do need to protect yourself.

Folks have gotten taken online to the tune of more than half a billion dollars a year, according to the Internet Crime

Complaint Center (ICCC), which is a joint government effort between the Federal Bureau of Investigation and the National White Collar Crime Center.

ICCC and other online security experts recommend that you take the following steps to protect yourself and your identity when conducting business online:

- ✔ Never access your bank accounts from a shared computer or on a shared network, such as the free access networks offered in hotel rooms and in other public or business facilities.

- ✔ Make certain that your computer has antivirus and firewall software that's periodically updated to keep up with the latest threats.

- ✔ Be aware of missed statements that could indicate your account has been taken over.

- ✔ Report unauthorized transactions to your bank or credit card company as soon as possible; otherwise, your bank may not stand behind the loss of funds.

- ✔ Use a complicated and unique password (including both letters and numbers) for your online bank account.

- ✔ Be careful about the sites you visit. Sites purporting to offer free access music, games, and movies are often sources of viruses and trojans that fraudsters use to steal your account information.

- ✔ Watch out for *phishers,* someone posing to be your bank or bank's representative. If "they" are contacting you, it's likely to be fraud. Never follow a bank link directly from an e-mail; always visit the bank Website directly by typing in the URL.

- ✔ Log out immediately after completing your transactions on financial Web sites.

Considering Your Alternatives

Other financial companies have similar — and in some cases even better — cost advantages than banks do, which translates into better deals for you. This section addresses two alternatives to bank accounts you may want to consider.

Brokerage accounts with check-writing

Brokerage firms enable you to buy and sell stocks, bonds, and other securities. Charles Schwab, Scottrade, E*Trade, TD Ameritrade, and Fidelity are among the larger brokerage firms or investment companies with substantial brokerage operations you may have read or heard about. (See Chapter 11 for my specific recommendations of firms that I like.)

Some of these firms have fairly extensive branch office networks and others don't. But those that have a reasonable number of branch offices have been able to keep a competitive position because of their extensive customer and asset base and because they aren't burdened by banking regulations (because they aren't banks) and the costs associated with operating as a bank.

A type of account worth checking out at brokerage firms is an *asset management account,* also referred to as a *cash management account.* Although the best deals on such accounts at some firms are only available to higher-balance investors, the best of these accounts typically enable you to

- ✔ Hold and invest in various investments (stocks, bonds, mutual funds, and so on) in a single account
- ✔ Write checks against a money market balance that pays competitive yields
- ✔ Use a Visa or MasterCard debit card for transactions

Money market funds

Basically, a *money market fund* is very similar to a bank savings account except that mutual fund companies offer them, which means they lack FDIC coverage. Historically, this hasn't been a problem, because retail money funds have never lost shareholder principal.

The attraction of money market funds is that the best ones pay higher yields than bank savings accounts and also come in tax-free versions, which is good for higher-tax-bracket investors. I explain money market funds in greater detail in Chapter 11.

Chapter 3

Budgeting and Saving

*U*nless you're the offspring of wealthy parents or grand-parents who have left you a sizable sum of money, you need to save money to accomplish your personal and financial goals. Early in your working years, saving money can be a challenge, of course. Although you're likely not earning a super-high income, you can live life and still buy the items (like a car and furniture) you need.

When you're first starting out, your salary is probably some-what low, and after fixed expenses (such as rent/mortgage, food, insurance, and so on), you may not have much money left for "fun" discretionary spending, let alone additional savings. Remember, though, that when it comes to building wealth, it doesn't matter what you make, it's what you spend and, therefore, are able to save. Many wealthy people didn't get rich based exclusively on their big salaries, but through disciplined savings and wise investing over time.

In this chapter, I discuss smart budgeting strategies and the tremendous long-term value that comes from regular saving and investing.

Developing a Savings Mind-Set

People typically learn their financial habits at a young age. During childhood, most people are exposed to messages and lessons about money, both at home with their parents and siblings and also in the world at large, such as at school and with their friends.

The expression "You can't teach an old dog new tricks" has some validity, at least for our four-legged friends, but even then, the expression actually requires some modification to be accurate. It should be, "It's hard to teach an old dog new tricks, but how hard it is depends on the dog."

My experiences have shown me the same to be true for people and their financial habits and decision making. For most people, spending money is easier and much more enjoyable than earning it. Of course, you can and should spend money, but there's a world of difference between spending money carelessly and spending money wisely.

I show you how to save money, even if you haven't been a good saver before. And even if you do think you're pretty good at saving, I have some tips and tricks so that you can get even better at saving more and spending less:

- ✔ **Live within your means.** Spending too much is a relative problem. If you spend $30,000 per year and your income is $40,000 annually, you should be in good shape and will be able to save a decent chunk of your income. But if your income is only $25,000 per year and you spend $30,000 annually, you'll be accumulating debt or spending from your investments to finance your lifestyle.

  How much you can safely spend while working toward your financial goals depends on what your goals are and where you are financially. At a minimum, you should be saving at least 5 percent of your gross annual (pretax) income, and ideally, you should save at least 10 percent.

- ✔ **Search for the best values.** The expression, "You get what you pay for," is an excuse for being a lazy shopper. The truth is that you can find high quality and low cost in the same product. Conversely, paying a high price is no guarantee that you're getting high quality. When you evaluate the cost of a product or service, think in terms of total, long-term costs. Buying a cheaper product only to spend a lot of additional money servicing and repairing it is no bargain. Research options and comparison shop to understand what's important to you. Don't waste money on bells and whistles that you don't need and might not ever use.

✔ **Don't assume brand names are the best.** Be suspicious of companies that spend gobs on image-oriented advertising. Branding is often used to charge premium prices. Blind taste tests have demonstrated that consumers can't readily discern quality differences between high- and low-cost brands with many products. Question the importance of the name and image of the products you buy. Companies spend a lot of money creating and cultivating an image, which has no impact on how their products taste or perform.

When you're grocery shopping, consider the store brand. Most of the time the ingredients are the same as the brand-name product (and may even be made by that same company). You don't need to shell out money to pay for the name.

✔ **Get your refunds.** Have you ever bought a product or service and didn't get what was promised? What did you do about it? Most people do nothing and let the company off the hook. Ask for your money back.

If you don't get satisfaction from a frontline employee, request to speak with a supervisor. If that fails and you bought the item with your credit or debit card, dispute the charge with the credit card company. You generally have up to 60 days to dispute and get your money back.

✔ **Trim your spending fat.** What you spend your money on is sometimes a matter of habit rather than a matter of what you really want or value. For example, some people shop at whatever stores are close to them. You need to set priorities and make choices about where you want and don't want to spend your money. See Chapter 4 for lots of tips for reducing your spending.

✔ **Turn your back on consumer credit.** Borrowing money to buy consumer items that depreciate (such as cars and electronics) is hazardous to your long-term financial health. Buy only what you can afford today. If you'll be forced to carry a debt on credit cards or an auto loan for months or years on end, you can't really afford what you're buying on credit today (see Chapter 18 for the details on saving on cars). The interest rate on consumer debt is generally high, and it isn't tax-deductible.

If you spend too much and spend unwisely, you put pressure on your income and your future need to continue working. Savings dwindle, debts may accumulate, and you won't be able to achieve your personal and financial goals.

What It's Worth: Valuing Savings over Time

Without a doubt, the amazing financial success stories get the headlines. You hear about company founders who make millions — sometimes billions — of dollars. Early investors in stocks such as Apple, Berkshire Hathaway, and Microsoft have made gargantuan returns. Who wouldn't want to make a return of 100 times, 200 times, or more on his investment?

However, expecting to make such king-sized returns is a recipe for disappointment and problems. (In Chapter 11, I discuss how to use the best investments in stocks, real estate, and small business to earn generous long-term returns.) The vast, vast majority of folks I've worked with and seen accumulate long-term wealth have done well because they regularly save money and they invest in somewhat riskier assets that produce expected long-term returns well above the rate of inflation, as the following section discusses.

The difference of continual savings

Okay, so you get that savings is important. How you save is equally important. Continually saving money on a regular basis rather than putting away a one-time savings can also generate larger returns.

For example, suppose you earn (after taxes) an extra $1,000 this year at a side job and you decide to save that money. In future years, you decide it's not worth the bother to do the extra work, so you're unable to save the money.

Now, compare that situation to one where you reduce your spending so that you can save $1,000 per year every year. In both cases, assume that you put the money in a savings account and earn 3 percent annually (which has been about the long-term average). Table 3-1 shows an example.

Table 3-1	Nest Egg Growth
Amount Saved	*Growth Potential*
One-time $1,000 saved	$3,260 after 40 years
$1,000 saved annually	$75,400 after 40 years

That's quite a stunning difference, huh? And that's just putting away the small amount of $1,000 annually. If you can put away $5,000 or $10,000 annually, then simply multiply the figures by 5 or 10.

The difference of a few percent return

When you save money, you want to try and get higher returns. Bonds, stocks, and other investment vehicles (check out Chapter 11) typically produce much better long-term average returns than a savings account or a certificate of deposit (CD), which usually offer a measly 3 percent annual return over the long term. The trade-off with the stocks, bonds, and such is that you must be able to withstand shorter-term declines in those investments' values.

If you put together a diversified portfolio of stocks and bonds, for example, you should be able to earn about 8 percent per year, on average, over the long term. You won't, of course, earn that amount every year — some years it will be less and some years it will be more. The following table shows how much you'd have after 40 years if you got a 3 percent annual return versus an 8 percent annual return.

Investment	*3% annual return*	*8% annual return*
One-time $1,000 saved	$3,260	$21,720
$1,000 saved annually	$75,400	$259,060

So when you combine regular saving with more-aggressive yet sensible investing, you end up with lots more money. Saving $1,000 yearly and getting just an average 8 percent annual return results in a nest egg of $259,060 in 40 years compared to ending up with just $3,260 if you invest $1,000 one time at 3 percent return over the same time period. And remember, if you can save more — such as $5,000 or $10,000 annually — you can multiply these numbers by 5 or 10.

With historic annual inflation running at about 3 percent, you're basically treading water if you're only earning a 3 percent investment return. As I discuss in Chapter 11, the goal of long-term investors is to grow the purchasing power of their portfolio, and that's where investments (such as stocks and bonds) with expected higher returns play a part.

Budgeting and Boosting Your Savings

When most people hear the word *budgeting,* they think unpleasant thoughts, like those associated with dieting, and rightfully so. Who wants to count calories or dollars and pennies? But *budgeting* — planning your future spending — can help you move from knowing how much you spend on various things to reducing your spending.

The following breaks down budgeting in simple steps:

1. **Analyze how and where you're currently spending.**

   Chapter 4 explains how to conduct your spending analysis.

2. **Calculate how much more you want to save each month.**

   Everyone has different goals. This book can help you develop yours and figure how much you should be saving to accomplish them.

3. **Determine where to make cuts in your spending.**

   Where you decide to cut is a personal decision. In Chapter 4, I provide plenty of ideas for how and where to make reductions.

Suppose that you're currently not saving any of your monthly income and you want to save 10 percent for retirement. If you can save and invest through a tax-sheltered retirement account — such as a 401(k), 403(b), SEP-IRA, or Keogh (see the section, "Valuing retirement accounts" later in this chapter) — then you don't actually need to cut your spending by 10 percent to reach a savings goal of 10 percent of your gross income.

When you contribute money to a tax-deductible retirement account, you reduce your federal and state taxes. If you're a moderate-income earner paying approximately 30 percent in federal and state taxes on your marginal income, you actually need to reduce your spending by only 7 percent to save 10 percent. The other 3 percent of the savings comes from the lowering of your taxes. (The higher your tax bracket, the less you need to cut your spending to reach a particular savings goal.)

So to boost your savings rate to 10 percent, you simply need to go through your current spending, category by category, until you come up with enough proposed cuts to reduce your spending by 7 percent. Make your cuts in areas that are the least painful and in areas where you're getting the least value from your current level of spending.

Considering another budgeting method

Another method of budgeting involves starting completely from scratch rather than examining your current expenses and making cuts from that starting point. Ask yourself how much you'd like to spend on different areas (such as rent, meals out, and so on).

The advantage of this approach is that it doesn't allow your current spending levels to constrain your thinking. Just because your current rent is $1,500 per month doesn't mean that it needs to remain there. When your current lease expires, you could change your housing arrangements and perhaps find a nice rental you can share with several others. I did this when I was fresh out of college, and doing so enabled me to keep my rent low and save more money.

You'll likely be amazed at the discrepancies between what you think you should be spending and what you actually are spending in certain categories. Take going out to eat, to bars, and to concerts, for example. You may think that spending $100 per month is reasonable and then discover that you've been averaging $250 per month in this category. Thus, you'd need to slash your spending here by 60 percent to get to your target.

If you don't have access to a tax-deductible retirement account or you're saving for other goals, budgeting still involves the same process of assessment and making cuts in various spending categories.

Setting and Prioritizing Your Savings Goals

You probably have some financial goals. If you don't, you should begin thinking about some financial goals you want to reach. Because everyone is unique, you surely have different goals than your parents, friends, neighbors, and siblings. Although goals may differ from person to person, accomplishing financial goals almost always requires saving money. In this section, I discuss common financial goals and how to work toward them.

Unless you earn a large income from your work or have a family inheritance to fall back on, your personal and financial desires probably outstrip your resources. Thus, you have to make choices.

Identifying common goals of accomplished savers

As a result of my experience counseling and teaching people about better personal financial management, I can share with you the common traits among folks who accomplish their goals. No matter how much money they made, the people I worked with who were the most successful were the ones who identified reasonable goals and worked toward them.

Among the common goals for folks in their 20s with whom I've worked are the following:

✔ **Making major purchases:** You need to plan for major purchases. So if you have a future purchase in mind for a car, living room furniture, vacation trips, and so on, you need to save toward that.

✔ **Owning a business:** Many people want to pursue the dream of starting and running their own business. The primary reason that most people continue just to dream is that they lack the money (and a specific plan) to leave their job. Although many businesses don't require gobs of start-up cash, almost all require that you withstand a substantial reduction in your income during the early years.

✔ **Buying a home:** Renting and dealing with landlords can be a financial and emotional drag, so most folks aspire to buy and own their own home. Despite the slide in property prices in the late 2000s, real estate has a pretty solid track record as a long-term investment. If you're looking to buy now or in the years ahead, the good news is that real estate is more affordable in most areas than it has been in a long, long time. (See Chapter 7 for more on housing.)

✔ **Starting a family/educating kids:** Having children leads some parents to cut back on work, which requires planning for living on a reduced income and facing higher expenses. And, if you have kids or are planning to have kids, you may want to help them get a college education. Unfortunately, that can cost a truckload of dough. Although you may never be in a position to cover all that cost, you'd probably like to be able to pay for a portion of it.

✔ **Retiring:** *Retiring* is a catchall term for discontinuing full-time work, or perhaps not even working for pay at all. You've probably just entered the workforce, but planning ahead for retirement is important. You may enjoy working and haven't given retirement much thought, but most people eventually do want to retire, and you want to be prepared. I address how to do that in the next section.

Valuing retirement accounts

Where possible, focus on saving and investing in accounts that offer you tax advantages. Retirement accounts — such as a 401(k), 403(b), SEP-IRA, Keogh, and so on — offer tax breaks to people of all economic means. In fact, lower-income and moderate-income earners have some additional tax breaks not available to higher-income earners. I discuss them later in this section.

Consider the following advantages to investing in retirement accounts:

✔ **Contributions are generally tax-deductible.** By putting money in a retirement account, you not only plan wisely for your future but also get an immediate financial reward: lower taxes. Paying less in taxes now means more money is available for saving and investing. Retirement account contributions are generally not taxed at either the federal or state income tax level until withdrawal (but they're still subject to Social Security and Medicare taxes when earned).

If you're paying, say, 30 percent between federal and state taxes (see Chapter 10 to determine your tax bracket and more details on tax-reduction strategies), a $5,000 contribution to a retirement account immediately lowers your income taxes by $1,500.

✔ **Returns on your investment compound over time without taxation.** After you put money into a retirement account, any interest, dividends, and appreciation add to your account without being taxed. Of course, there's no such thing as a free lunch; these accounts don't generally allow for complete tax avoidance. (Health Savings Accounts, which I discuss in Chapter 13, can offer complete tax avoidance. Also, though it offers no upfront tax breaks, the Roth IRA, which I discuss in Chapter 10, enables future tax-free withdrawals.) Yet you can get a really great lunch at a discount: You get to defer taxes on all the accumulating gains and profits until you withdraw the money down the road. Thus, more money is working for you over a longer period of time.

✔ **Lower-income earners can get a special tax credit.** In addition to the tax breaks I discuss previously, U.S. tax laws also provide a special tax *credit,* which is a percentage (ranging from 10 to 50 percent) of the first $2,000 contributed (or $4,000 on a joint return) to a retirement account. Unlike a deduction, a tax credit directly reduces your tax bill by the amount of the credit. The credit isn't available to those under the age of 18, full-time students, or people who are claimed as dependents on someone else's tax return.

Married couples filing jointly with adjusted gross incomes (AGIs) of less than $55,500 and single taxpayers with an adjusted gross income of less than $27,750 can earn this retirement saver's tax credit (claimed on Form 8880) for retirement account contributions.

✔ **Matching money may be available.** In some company retirement accounts, companies match a portion of your own contributions. Thus, in addition to tax breaks, you get free extra money (terms vary by company) courtesy of your employer. But you have to contribute some of your own money to get the matching money. If you don't, you're essentially throwing away money, which is never a good thing to do!

Dealing with competing goals

Unless you enjoy paying higher taxes, you may wonder why you'd choose to save money outside of retirement accounts, which shelter your money from taxation. The reason is that some financial goals aren't readily achieved by saving in retirement accounts. Also, retirement accounts have caps on the amount you can contribute annually and restrictions for accessing the account.

Because you're constrained by your financial resources, you need to prioritize your goals. Before funding your retirement accounts and racking up those tax breaks, you should consider your other goals, such as starting or buying a business or buying a home.

If you withdraw funds from traditional retirement accounts before age 59½ and you're not retired, you not only have to pay income taxes on the withdrawals but also usually have to pay early withdrawal penalties — 10 percent of the withdrawn amount in federal tax, plus whatever your state charges. So if you're accumulating money for a down payment on a home or to start or buy a business, you probably should save that money outside of a retirement account so that you get penalty-free access to the funds.

Saving When You're Strapped

You know that putting aside some money on a regular basis is important, but you may wonder how realistic it is, especially when you're burdened with a never-ending list of bills or are first starting out on your own. And, those six-figure per year jobs haven't yet come your way! So what do you do? The first and most important thing is to work at paying down high-cost debt (see Chapter 5).

You can get into the habit of saving even when your income is low. Even if you can set aside just $5 or $10 every paycheck, you're on the road. As you earn raises or bonuses, you can increase the amount you save. The bottom line: Put a little in savings on a regular basis.

You may consider getting a part-time job. You can put the money you make from this second job right into savings. Don't even touch it. If you decide to get a part-time job, make sure that it's something you enjoy so you don't end up dreading it. If you're strapped and barely making ends meet, you can also cut expenses. Chapter 4 has tips on reducing your spending.

Chapter 4

How to Spend Less and Save More

· ·

In This Chapter

▶ Managing your housing costs and taxes

▶ Handling food, transportation, fashion, and recreation expenses

▶ Containing your technology, insurance, professional advice, and healthcare spending

· ·

*W*hen I worked as a financial counselor, I was surprised at how often clients solicited my feedback on their spending, because a good portion of them were doing a fine job saving money. In addition to wanting to know how to save more to accomplish their goals, they also wanted to know how their spending compared to others and how they could best cut their own spending.

This chapter includes the same advice I gave my clients about spending money. How and where you spend your money is a matter of personal choice and priorities, but those choices can affect the amount of money you have to save. In this chapter, I present ideas on how to get the most from spending and how to spend less. (In Chapter 3, I discuss the importance of developing a savings mind-set, as well as budgeting and spending strategies.)

Hemming Housing Costs

Housing and its associated costs such as insurance, utilities, furniture, maintenance, and repairs (for homeowners) are the largest or second-largest expenditure for most people. If you can keep these costs (and taxes) under control, which I explain how to do in this section, you'll go a long way toward being able to save some money.

Containing rental costs

When you're in your early 20s and you don't have dependents, living in a low-cost fashion is easier than it is later in life. The living arrangements may have some downsides, but young single people tend to have a broader range of rental options than those available to married people with kids.

The late 2000s decline in home prices coupled with low interest rates have made housing the most affordable it has been in decades. That's great news if you're a renter looking to become a future homeowner, or if you simply want to rent a nicer dwelling. Of course, each local market is unique, and if you happen to live in an area with a strong, diverse economy and little developable land or excess housing, your local housing market may be stronger and more expensive than most others. Turn to Chapter 7 for more information on buying real estate.

The following sections point out what you can do to minimize your rent expense and associated costs.

Live with relatives

Yes, I fully realize that living with relatives won't work for some families. However, if your folks or other relatives have the space and temperament to let you live under their roof, it can be a terrific way to keep your rental costs to a minimum. Just be sure to have some lengthy discussions first to set expectations and ground rules, raise concerns, and establish terms, including costs and rental agreements.

Share a rental with roommates

Living solo is a pricey luxury most younger people can't afford. Doing so definitely has its benefits — you have more privacy and control over your home environment. Renting may sacrifice some of these advantages to living alone, but having roomies also has its pros. If you share a rental with roommates, the per-person costs should be substantially less than if you live solo. You must be in a sharing mood, though, to live harmoniously with roommates. They may help themselves to your food or shampoo, stay up late when you need to get up early the next day, or invite over inconsiderate friends. Roommates aren't all bad, though, as they can brighten your social life.

Before you choose to share a dwelling with someone, make sure that you can live with the person for the length of the rental agreement. If you break the lease, you may owe a hefty amount of money, which defeats the purpose of saving money with a roommate.

Be sure to have a rental agreement in place with your landlord and to have all renters listed in the agreement. Don't allow others who aren't listed in the agreement to live in the rental, because you and the other renters could be on the hook for damage they cause and rent they don't pay.

Move to a lower-cost rental

You may realize that you're currently living beyond your means and you need to make some adjustments. You may have allowed your champagne tastes to exceed your beer budget when you went shopping for a home rental. So long as you're completing your current lease, there's no reason you can't move to a lower-cost rental. The less you spend renting, the more you can save toward buying your own place. Just be sure to factor in all the costs of moving to and living in a new rental.

Of course, a lower-cost rental may be lower quality and not up to your standards. Don't accept living in a high-crime neighborhood, a poorly maintained building, or a location that causes you to burn much of your free time commuting to work.

Negotiate your rental increases

Every year, some landlords increase their tenants' rent no matter how good the tenant has been and regardless of the state of the economy. If your local economy is soft (check out the unemployment rate) and the rental market is soft or your living quarters are deteriorating, negotiate with your landlord. You have more leverage and power than you probably realize. A smart landlord doesn't want to lose good tenants who pay rent on time. Filling vacancies takes time and money.

State your case through a well-crafted and polite note or personal visit. Explain how you have been a responsible tenant, always paid your rent on time, and cared for your unit, and convey that your research shows comparable rentals going for less. Briefly explaining any challenging financial circumstances (such as reduced pay from your job) may help your case as well. If you can't stave off the rent increase, perhaps you can negotiate some improvements you value.

Get on the path to purchasing your own home

Purchasing a home always seems costly. However, over the long term, owning is usually less costly than renting a similar property. And as a homeowner, you build *equity* (the difference between the home's value and what you owe on it) in your property as you make mortgage payments and the home's value increases over the long term. If you purchase a property with a 30-year fixed-rate mortgage, the biggest expense of ownership — your monthly mortgage payment — is locked in and remains level. By contrast, as a renter, unless you live in a rent-controlled unit, your entire monthly housing cost is exposed to inflation.

Slicing homeowner expenses

If you own a home or are about to buy one, you can take many steps to keep your ownership costs down and under control without neglecting your property or living like a pauper. The following sections are my tips.

Buy a home that fits your budget

Purchase a home that you can afford. During the booming real estate market of the early to mid-2000s, getting overextended with debt was pretty easy. You didn't need a decent-size down payment or even have to have your income verified to buy a home if you made a larger down payment. Furthermore, interest-only loans allowed borrowers to shrink their mortgage payments by delaying repayment of any of their principal.

I was never a fan of such loans, which is why in our bestselling book *Home Buying For Dummies* (Wiley), my coauthor Ray Brown and I advise that the best way to buy a home is to examine your budget and financial resources before shopping for a home. As the real estate market crashed in the late 2000s, some of those people who bought homes that stretched their budgets lost their homes to foreclosure because they got in over their head, fell on hard times, and couldn't afford their monthly mortgage payments.

Even if you can afford the monthly mortgage payment on a house you're looking to buy, if you have too little money left over for your other needs and wants — such as taking trips, eating out, going to concerts, enjoying hobbies, or saving for retirement — your dream home may become a financial prison. See Chapter 7 for help in figuring how much you can afford to spend monthly on a home and still accomplish your other goals.

Get a roommate (and some rental income)

Owning a home can be much more affordable if you have some monthly rental coming in. Consider renting a bedroom to a roommate who can pay monthly rent as well as help with utilities.

If you decide to get a roommate, make sure that you check the renter thoroughly through references and a credit report, and be sure to discuss ground rules and expectations before sharing your space. Also, ask your insurance company to see whether your homeowner's policy needs adjustments to cover potential liability from renting.

Contain your utility costs

You can take steps to keep your utility costs down whether you own or rent a home. First, don't waste energy, even if you don't pay for it out of pocket as a renter. Landlords absolutely factor your energy consumption into future rental-hike decisions. Paying for your own utilities should get you to consider wearing layers in the winter and not expecting your home to feel like a meat locker in the heat of summer.

Especially if you have to pay for garbage service, recycle as much as possible. Seek the replacement of old, energy-guzzling appliances and where possible, beef up your property's insulation. Obviously, if you're a renter, you have no control over these things but you should certainly ask.

Cutting Your Taxes

Alongside the costs of owning or renting a home, taxes are the other large personal expenditure for most folks. Everyone gets socked with taxes when earning income and when investing and spending money. That's the bad news — the good news is that you can reduce the amount of taxes you pay by using some relatively simple yet powerful strategies. The following two tax trimmers can help; Chapter 10 has more tax-reduction strategies.

- ✔ **Utilize retirement savings plans.** To take advantage of such plans, you must spend less than you earn. Only then can you afford to contribute to these plans.

- ✔ **Reduce the amount of sales tax you pay.** To do so, you must spend less and save more. When you buy most consumer products, you pay sales tax. Therefore, if you spend less money and save more in retirement accounts, you reduce your income and sales taxes.

Managing Food Costs

Not eating is one way to reduce food expenditures; however, this method isn't very realistic. The following culinary strategies can keep you on your feet — perhaps even improve your health — and help you save money.

- ✔ **Discover how to cook.** Take a course and read some good books on cooking. Consider that most people eat three meals a day, 365 days a year. That's more than 1,000 meals yearly — a lot of eating! If you don't know how to cook for yourself and how to do so healthfully, you may end up spending a lot more money on food and eating out — and have poor health to boot. What you don't eat, you can put in the refrigerator or freezer and eat at a later meal. Making your own food saves you money, helps you enjoy your food more, and makes you more attractive to a mate!

- ✔ **Consider store brands.** Name-brand companies spend a lot of money on advertising and marketing, which you, the consumer, end up paying for through higher prices. You can save a considerable amount of money by buying the store brand, which is usually the same quality (and sometimes the same product) as the name brand at a lower price.

✔ **Buy in bulk.** You can save substantially by shopping at stores that are able to sell groceries for less because of their operating efficiencies. Topping that list are wholesale superstores such as Costco and Sam's Club. The catch is that you must buy most items in bulk or in larger sizes. An additional advantage to buying in bulk: It requires fewer shopping trips (hence less gasoline) and results in fewer instances of running out of things.

If you decide to buy in bulk, be careful with items that can spoil. Make sure that you buy what you can reasonably use (or freeze when necessary). If you're single, shop with a friend and split the order. If you're looking for a store that sells more organic and natural products at a reasonable price and in smaller sizes, check out Trader Joe's.

✔ **Kick the bottled water habit.** Although tap water often does leave something to be desired, lab analysis of bottled water shows it has its own problems. You can save hundreds of dollars annually and drink cleaner water by installing a water filtration system at home and improving your tap (or well) water. See `www.erictyson.com` for more details.

✔ **Pack your lunch sometimes.** Eating out daily can rack up a lot of expense.

✔ **Spend carefully when dining out.** Eating out can be a lot of fun, but keep in mind that you're essentially hiring someone to shop, cook, and clean up for you! You can save some money when eating out by remembering these points:

- **Eat out for breakfast or lunch rather than dinner.** You can generally get the most bang for your buck then.

- **Go easy on the beverages.** Alcohol is especially expensive when dining out.

- **Gravitate toward the dishes that cost less.** Vegetarian dishes cost less than premium meat-based entrées (and are generally healthier for you).

Trimming Transportation Expenses

When you're considering the cost of living in different areas, don't forget to factor in commuting costs. Getting to and fro on a daily basis can get expensive if you don't keep an eye on your expenses. Many people rely on cars for their transportation. Buying and operating a car can be a tremendous financial burden, especially if you borrow to buy or lease the car. You can control your transportation costs by following my suggestions:

- **Opt for public transportation.** Choose to live in an area that offers reliable public transportation, such as a subway or bus system. You can often purchase monthly passes at a reasonable rate. If you live close to work, or at least close to a public transit system, you may be able to make do with fewer cars (or no car at all) in your household.

- **Ride your bike.** During warmer months, consider jumping on your bike to get around. You can save money and get some exercise. Just be sure to be safe!

- **If you must have a car, look at cheaper options than financing or leasing one.** Having provided financial advice to many folks over many years, I can tell you from direct observation that spending on cars is one of the leading causes of overspending and undersaving. I understand that in some parts of the United States and Canada, going without a car is nearly impossible, and I also understand that driving a car is a wonderful convenience that I have personally enjoyed during most of my adult life.

  But if you can avoid having your own car, by all means do so. You can also consider renting a car when needed if you don't find yourself wanting to use one frequently.

  The main reason people end up spending more than they can afford on a car is that they finance the purchase. When buying a car, you should buy one you can afford with cash, which for many people means buying a good-quality used car. Check out Chapter 18 for more helpful advice.

When shopping for a car, don't make the mistake of simply comparing sticker prices. Consider the total long-term costs of car ownership, which include gas, insurance, registration fees, maintenance, repairs, and taxes (sales and personal property). And be sure to consider the safety of any car you buy, as driving is surely the most dangerous thing you do. See the National Highway Traffic Safety Administration's Web site (`www.safercar.gov`), which has lots of crash-test data, as well as information on other car-safety issues.

Finessing Fashion Finances

The good news for you as a consumer is that in the fashion industry, global competition has driven down prices for consumers. Here's what you can do to look like a million bucks (on and off the job) while spending fewer of your bucks:

- ✔ **Don't chase the latest fashions.** Ignore publications and ads that splash celebrities wearing the latest looks. You don't need to buy lots of new clothes every year. If your clothes aren't lasting at least ten years, you're probably tossing them before their time or buying clothing that isn't very durable. Of course, when you enter an office job for the first time, you're probably going to have to buy some new clothing. True fashion, as defined by what people wear, changes quite slowly. In fact, the classics never go out of style. If you want the effect of a new wardrobe every year, store last year's purchases away next year and then bring them out the year after. Or rotate your clothing inventory every third year. Set your own fashion standards.

- ✔ **Shun dry cleaning–required clothing.** Stick with cottons and machine-washable synthetics rather than wools or silks that require costly dry cleaning.

- ✔ **Consider buying gently used fashion at consignment shops, vintage shops, or online.** You can find great bargains at these places that others may have worn only once or twice and didn't like.

- ✔ **Look for deep discounts.** Many stores have a once-a-year huge sale with major price reductions. Pay close attention for big sales.

> ✔ **Minimize accessories.** Shoes, jewelry, handbags, and the like can gobble large amounts of money. Again, how many of these accessory items do you really need? The answer is probably very few, because each one should last many years. Don't purchase accessories and then not use them.

Recreating on a Budget

Having fun and taking time out for recreation can be money well spent. However, you can easily engage in financial extravagance, which can wreck an otherwise good budget. Here are my favorite tips for getting the most from your recreation spending:

> ✔ **Don't equate spending (more) money with having (more) fun.** Many movies, theaters, museums, and restaurants offer discount prices on certain days and times. Cultivate some interests and hobbies that are free or low cost. Visiting with friends, hiking, reading, and playing sports can be good for your finances as well as your health.

> ✔ **Hang out with people who share your values and aren't material.** It's especially important that you find a partner who isn't a spendthrift and isn't overly impressed with material things.

> ✔ **Take vacations you can afford.** Don't borrow on credit cards to finance your travels. Try taking shorter vacations that are closer to home. For example, have you been to a state or national park recently? Take a vacation at home, visiting the sites in your local area. For longer distance travel, go during the off-season and off-peak times and days for the best deals on airfares and hotels.

Taming Technology Spending

It seems there's no end of ways to stay in touch and be entertained, as well as a never-ending stream of new gadgets. Although I enjoy choices and convenience as much as the next person, the cost for all these services and gadgets adds up, leading to a continued enslavement to your career. Err on the side of keeping your life simple. Doing so costs less, reduces stress, and allows more time for the things that really do matter in life.

Keep the following in mind before you spend money on technology:

- ✔ **Especially when it comes to new technology and gadgets, wait.** You don't have to be the first person to get something new. When something new first hits the market, prices are relatively high and the gadget inevitably has bugs. Wait at least a couple of years and your patience will be rewarded with much lower prices and more reliable products. Also, do your homework before going shopping. Consumer Reports and CNET (www. cnet.com) are useful resources.

- ✔ **Be aware of how much you spend on your cellphone.** Cellphones are a particular device that can encourage the wasting of money. Of course, if your employer pays for your cellphone as a perk, you can skip what I have to say on this topic. In addition to downloads, text messaging, Web surfing, and other services, you can find all sorts of entertaining ways to run up huge cellphone bills each month. Ask yourself whether you really need all these costly bells and whistles.

If you don't use your phone a lot, consider a prepaid plan where you pay only for what you use. If you typically use a few hundred minutes per month or fewer, you should save money with one of these plans. Last but not least, be safe with your cellphone, especially when driving, and don't hold a cellphone to your ear when talking because of long-term health concerns about the radiation emitted from these phones.

Keeping Down Insurance Costs

Insurance is a big area — so big, in fact, that Part IV of this book covers it in detail. The following tips help you minimize your insurance spending while making the most of it:

- ✔ **Utilize high deductibles.** Each insurance policy has a *deductible,* which is the amount of a loss that must come out of your pocket before coverage kicks in. Higher deductibles can help to greatly lower your premiums. However, if you have a lot of claims, you won't come out ahead with lower deductibles, because your insurance premiums will escalate.

- ✓ **Obtain broad coverage.** Don't buy insurance for anything that won't be a financial catastrophe if you have to pay for it out of your own pocket. For example, buying simple dental or home warranty plans, which cover relatively small potential expenditures, doesn't make financial sense. And if no one's dependent on your income, you don't need life insurance, either. (Who'll be around to collect when you're gone?)

- ✓ **Always shop around.** Rates vary tremendously among insurers. For each of the major insurance policies, I provide you with a short list of the best companies to call for quotes and other cost-saving strategies in Part IV.

- ✓ **Take care of your health.** Exercise at least a few times per week and eat healthfully. You only get one body and one chance to take care of it.

Getting Professional Advice

Although your life may be relatively simple now, sometimes you may have to deal with new challenges, and you may benefit from a seasoned pro at your side. Tax, legal, business, and financial advisors can be worth more than their expense if they know what they're doing and you pay a reasonable fee. Here's how to get the most out of your spending when you hire advisors:

- ✓ **Get educated first.** How can you possibly evaluate an expert on a certain topic if you don't know much about the topic yourself? Reading this book, for example, is an excellent thing to do before hiring a financial advisor. Printed and software-based resources can be useful, low-cost alternatives and supplements to hiring professionals.

- ✓ **Use professionals only when needed — not constantly.** Most people most of the time should hire a professional only on an as-needed basis. But be wary of professionals who create or perpetuate work and have conflicts of interest with their recommendations.

> ✔ **Scrutinize and interview thoroughly before hiring.** Do background research to evaluate each prospective advisor's strengths and biases. Be sure to check references and conduct an Internet search to see what you can find out about the person. Check regulatory associations in your state for any citations or actions taken against an advisor.

Chapter 17 provides you more information about different types of professionals you can hire.

Handling Healthcare Expenses

When you're young and in good health, you usually don't give much thought to healthcare expenses and health insurance. But you have health insurance for a reason, and unfortunately, the cost of healthcare continues to rise faster than the overall rate of inflation. Use these tips to protect yourself:

✔ **Shop around for health insurance and healthcare.** Many different plan designs are available with a wide variation in costs. Also, like any other profession, medical providers have a profit motive, so they may recommend something that isn't your best option. Don't take any one physician's advice as gospel. Always get a second opinion for any major surgery.

✔ **Examine your employer's benefit plans.** Take advantage of being able to put away a portion of your income before taxes to pay for out-of-pocket healthcare expenses, especially in health savings accounts (see Chapter 13).

✔ **Investigate alternative medicine and tread carefully.** Alternative medicine's focus on preventive care and treatment of the whole body or person are pluses.

Just keep your antenna up for pie-in-the-sky promises and charlatans out to empty your wallet. Check with your physician before trying any alternatives.

✔ **Kick your addictions.** Smoking, alcohol, drugs, and gambling can cost you financially and emotionally. Be honest with yourself about the damage that excesses in these areas is causing in your life and take action now to get on a healthier path.

Chapter 5

Using Loans and Paying Down Debts

In This Chapter

▶ Understanding the best uses for debt

▶ Strategies for paying off debt

▶ Seeking relief from extreme debt

*B*orrowing money and taking on debt is like using a chainsaw. With proper training and safety precautions, a chainsaw can be a useful tool. In the hands of an insufficiently trained user or when used in the wrong situations, this useful tool can do serious damage. The same can be said for borrowing money. Used sensibly, loans can help you accomplish important goals and boost your net worth over time. Unfortunately, taking on debt can also cause problems: living beyond your means, borrowing against your future earnings, and lowering your longer-term net worth.

In this chapter, I help you understand the best uses for loans and what debts to avoid. I also explain how to conquer the all-too-common problem of consumer debt.

Eyeing the Causes of Generational Debt

For a number of years now, it has been argued that young adults are under pressures that lead them to dig deeper into debt than prior generations. The reasons cited for this *generational debt* have typically included

✔ **High costs of college:** Annual increases in the costs of a college education have far outstripped the increases in general prices of other products and services.

✔ **Stagnating incomes and job prospects:** Most industries and companies compete in an increasingly global economy. The severe recession of the late 2000s has led to a tighter than normal job market.

✔ **High housing costs:** The 1990s and most of the 2000s saw rapidly rising housing prices, which priced many entry-level buyers out of their local markets.

✔ **College campus credit card promotions:** The availability and promotion of credit cards is a big problem. Credit cards are tempting to use during college when your income is minimal or nonexistent. On many college and university campuses, banks are allowed, through payment of large fees to the education institution, to promote their credit cards. This practice is getting more and more young people hooked on credit cards at younger ages.

✔ **More temptations to spend money:** Never before have so many temptations existed for spending money through so many outlets. In addition to the ubiquity of retail stores, people are bombarded with online ads.

Most of these reasons are valid now, except for the one about housing costs. The severe recession of the late 2000s knocked down housing prices pretty significantly in most areas. Those lower prices, combined with historically low interest rates, have made housing the most affordable it has been in decades in most areas.

You may encounter some or all of these debt traps during your 20s. Remember that you'll always face things in life that you can and can't control. If you're aware of these traps and can discern the difference between what you can't control and what you can constructively do to contain your spending and debt, then you're on the right track. If certain venues or situations or people tempt you to overreach, then avoid them. The rest of this chapter can help you get started.

Making the Most of Loans

Not all debt is bad. In fact, some debt can help you better your life and may even pay off in the long run. Taking out a loan for the right reasons can make good financial sense because you're making an investment. Loans for your education, for buying or starting a small business, or for buying real estate can give you a return on your investment. Furthering your education, for example, should increase your income-earning ability. Borrowing to invest in a good piece of real estate or a small business should pay off over the years as well. Despite the potential, however, there's no guarantee that you'll earn a return above and beyond your loan's interest costs.

Borrowing and taking on debt for consumption — such as for buying a new car, new furniture, or electronics, or for a costly vacation trip — isn't a good financial idea because such borrowing encourages living beyond your means. And the interest on consumer debt is generally not tax-deductible and carries a higher rate than the interest on investment debt. (Check out the next section for tips on how to eliminate your consumer debt.)

Working Off Consumer Debt

You accumulate *consumer debt* (credit card debt, auto loan debts, and so on) when your expenses exceed your income. Therefore, it stands to reason that to pay off consumer debt, you need to decrease your spending (see Chapter 4) and/or increase your income. Slowing down the growth of your debt can also assist. The following sections help you jump-start getting rid of your consumer debt.

Kicking the credit card habit

With their wide acceptance by merchants and their ease of use, credit cards foster living beyond your means by extending credit. That's why I recommend that you cut up all your credit cards and call the card issuers to cancel your accounts if you've had a habit of accumulating debt on credit cards.

You can manage your finances and expenditures without having a credit card. Now, if you can trust yourself to be responsible, keep one credit card only for new purchases that you know you can absolutely pay in full each month. But if you decide to keep one widely accepted credit card instead of getting rid of them all, be careful. You may be tempted to let debt accumulate and roll over for a month or two, starting up the whole horrible process of running up your consumer debt again. Even better than keeping one credit card is getting a debit card (see the next section).

If you're not going to take my advice to get rid of all your credit cards or secure a debit card, be sure to keep a lid on your credit card's credit limit (the maximum balance allowed on your card). You don't have to accept a higher limit just because your bank keeps raising your credit limit to reward you for being such a profitable customer. Call your credit card service's toll-free phone number and lower your credit limit to a level you're comfortable with.

Discovering debit cards: Convenience without credit temptation

Just because you get rid of your credit cards doesn't mean you have to start carrying your checkbook or large amounts of cash around with you. Enter the debit card, which offers you the convenience of making purchases with a piece of plastic without the temptation or ability to run up credit card debt. A debit card looks just like a credit card with either the Visa or MasterCard logo. Debit cards have the following characteristics, which are different from credit cards:

- ✔ **Deduction from checking account:** As with checks, debit card purchase amounts are deducted electronically from your checking account within days. By contrast, if you pay your credit card bill in full and on time each month, your credit card gives you free use of the money you owe until it's time to pay the bill.

- ✔ **Potential for overdrawing checking account:** If you switch to a debit card and you keep your checking account balance low and don't ordinarily balance your checkbook, you may need to start balancing it. Otherwise, you may face unnecessary bounced check charges. (*Overdraft protection* may be worth considering, but beware of the temptation to use that as an ongoing, high-interest credit line on balances borrowed, similar to a credit card.)

✔ **Shorter window time for making disputes:** Credit cards make it easier for you to dispute charges for problematic merchandise through the issuing bank. Most banks allow you to dispute charges for up to 60 days after purchase and will credit the disputed amount to your account, pending resolution. Most debit cards offer a much shorter window, typically less than one week, for making disputes. (Despite widespread misperception, personal debit cards have identical fraud protection as personal credit cards.)

If you don't already have a debit card, ask your current bank whether it offers Visa or MasterCard debit cards. If your bank doesn't offer one, shop among the major banks in your area, which are likely to offer such debit cards. As debit cards come with checking accounts, do some comparison shopping between the different account features and fees. Check out Chapter 2 for more information about finding the right bank for you.

Also check out getting a Visa or MasterCard debit card with the asset management accounts offered by investment firms. *Asset management accounts* basically are accounts that combine your investments, such as stocks, bonds, and mutual funds, with a transaction account. One drawback of these accounts is that most of them require fairly hefty minimum initial investment amounts — typically $5,000 to $10,000. Among brokerages with competitive investment offerings and prices are TD Ameritrade (800-934-4448; www.tdameritrade.com), Vanguard (800-992-8327; www.vanguard.com), and Muriel Siebert (800-872-0711; www.siebertnet.com).

Lowering your credit card's interest rate

If you do have credit card debt, you can slow its growth until you get it paid off by reducing the interest rate you're paying. Here are some methods for doing that:

✔ **Stop making new charges on cards that have outstanding balances while you're paying down your credit card balance(s).** Many people don't realize that interest starts to accumulate immediately when they carry a balance. You have no *grace period,* the 20 or so days you normally have to pay your balance in full without incurring interest charges, if you carry a credit card balance month to month.

✔ **Apply for a lower-rate credit card.** To qualify, you need a top-notch credit report and score (see Chapter 6), and not too much debt outstanding relative to your income. After you're approved for a new, lower-interest-rate card, simply transfer your outstanding balance from your higher-rate card.

See my Web site, www.erictyson.com, for an up-to-date list of good, low-rate cards.

As you shop for a low-interest-rate credit card, be sure to check out all the terms and conditions of each card. Start by reviewing the uniform rates and terms of disclosure, which details the myriad fees and conditions (especially how much your interest rate could increase for missed or late payments). Also understand how the future interest rate is determined on cards that charge variable interest rates.

Negotiating better rates from your current credit card

Rather than transferring your current credit card balance onto a lower-interest-rate card, you can try to negotiate a better deal from your current credit card company. Start by calling the bank that issued your current, high-interest-rate credit card and inform the bank that you want to cancel your card because you found a competitor that offers no annual fee and a lower interest rate. Your bank may choose to match the terms of the "competitor" rather than lose you as a customer. If it doesn't,

get that application completed for a lower-rate card.

Be careful with this strategy, and consider just paying off or transferring the balance without actually canceling the higher-interest-rate credit card. Canceling the card, especially if it's one you've had for a number of years, may lower your credit score. Just be sure not to run up new charges on the card you're transferring the balance from.

Tapping investments to reduce consumer debt

If you have savings and investment balances available to pay off consumer debt, like high-interest credit card debt and auto loans, consider doing so. Pay off the loans with the highest interest rates first. Although your savings and investments may be earning decent returns, the interest you're paying on your consumer debts is likely higher. Paying off consumer loans on a credit card at, say, 14 percent is like finding an investment with a guaranteed return of 14 percent — tax-free. You'd actually need to find an investment that yielded even more — around 21 percent if you're in a moderate tax bracket — to net 14 percent after paying taxes in order to justify not paying off your 14 percent loans. The higher your tax bracket (explained in Chapter 10), the higher the return you need on your investments to justify keeping high-interest consumer debt. (This discussion refers to investments in nonretirement accounts. Unless your tax bracket drops because of an extended layoff from work or from going back to school, withdrawing money from retirement accounts is costly because of the requirement to pay current federal and state income taxes on the amount withdrawn, not to mention penalties.)

When using your savings to pay down consumer debts, leave yourself enough cash to be in a position to withstand an unexpected large expense or temporary loss of income.

Paying down balances

If you've been reading this chapter from the beginning, you know that I discuss numerous strategies for zapping your consumer debt. Let's take the discussion a level deeper. How do you handle paying down multiple consumer-debt balances? It's really pretty simple *after* you implement the advice I give up until this point in the chapter.

After meeting the minimum required monthly payment terms for each loan, I strongly advocate that you channel extra payments toward paying down those loans with the highest interest rate first. The financial benefit of doing so should be obvious. If you have one loan at a 20 percent annual interest cost and another at an 8 percent annual interest cost, you'll be saving yourself a 12 percent annual interest cost by paying down the higher-cost loan faster.

I'm amazed at the wrong-headed advice I continue to see on this topic, especially on the Internet. One guru with no discernible training in the financial-planning/personal-finance field advocates the "snowball method" of debt reduction. He advises that you rank your debt payments by their total outstanding balances and that you channel extra payments to those with the lowest total balance owed. The "theory" behind this is that the psychological boost from paying down smaller debts completely will lead you to keep paying down your other debts.

In my real-world experience as a financial counselor, I've found folks to be intelligent and more responsive to the psychological rewards of saving money. And you best save money by paying down your highest-interest debts first.

Getting Help for Extreme Debt

More drastic action may be required if you have significant debts or simply are overwhelmed with what to do about it. In this section I discuss getting help from a credit counseling agency and the last-resort option of bankruptcy.

Seeking counseling

If you're seriously in debt, you may consider a credit counselor. The ads for these agencies are everywhere. Although some of these organizations do a decent job, many are effectively funded by the fees that creditors pay them. Before you hire a credit counseling agency, make sure you do your research on the company.

Put together a list of questions to ask to find a credit counseling agency that meets your needs. Here are some key questions you can ask:

> ✔ **Do you offer debt management programs?** In a *debt management program (DMP),* a counseling agency puts you on a repayment plan with your creditors and gets paid a monthly fee for handling the payments. You

should avoid agencies offering DMPs because of conflicts of interest. An agency can't offer objective advice about all your options for dealing with debt, including bankruptcy, if it has a financial incentive to put you on a DMP.

This creates a bias in their counsel to place debt-laden folks seeking their advice on their debt management programs wherein the consumer agrees to pay a certain amount per month to the agency, which in turn parcels out the money to the various creditors. Agencies typically recommend that debtors go on a repayment plan that has the consumer pay, say, 3 percent of each outstanding loan balance to the agency, which in turn pays the money to creditors.

Although credit counseling agencies' promotional materials and counselors highlight the drawbacks to bankruptcy, counselors are reluctant to discuss the negative impact of signing up for a debt payment plan.

✔ **What are your fees, including setup and/or monthly fees?** Get a specific price quote and contract in writing. Avoid any credit counseling service that charges a high upfront fee before it provides any services. And watch out if the service tells you to stop paying your bills; it may take your money and run while your credit gets ruined.

✔ **Are you licensed to offer your services in my state?** You should only work with an agency licensed to operate in your state.

✔ **What are the qualifications of your counselors?** Are they accredited or certified by an outside organization? If so, by whom? If not, how are they trained? Try to use an organization whose counselors are trained by a nonaffiliated party.

✔ **What assurance do I have that information about me will be kept confidential and secure?** This information includes your address, phone number, and financial information. Reputable agencies provide clearly written privacy policies.

✔ **How are your employees compensated?** Are they paid more if I sign up for certain services, if I pay a fee, or if I make a contribution to your organization? Employees who work on an incentive basis are less likely to have your best interests in mind than those who earn a straight salary that isn't influenced by your choices.

Considering bankruptcy

When the amount of your high-interest consumer debt relative to your annual income exceeds 25 percent, filing bankruptcy may be your best option. Like any tool, it has its pros and cons.

Bankruptcy's potential advantages include the following:

✔ **Certain debts can be completely eliminated or discharged.** Debts that typically can be discharged include credit card, medical, auto, utilities, and rent. Eliminating your debt also allows you to start working toward your financial goals, such as saving to purchase a home or toward retirement. Depending on the amount of outstanding debt you have relative to your income, you may need a decade or more to pay it all off.

Debts that may not be canceled through bankruptcy generally include child support, alimony, student loans, taxes, and court-ordered damages (for example, drunk driving settlements).

✔ **Certain assets are protected by bankruptcy.** In every state, you can retain certain property and assets when you file for bankruptcy. Most states allow you to protect a certain amount of home equity; some states allow you to keep your home regardless of its value. Additionally, you're allowed to retain some other types and amounts of personal property and assets. For example, most states allow you to retain household furnishings, clothing, pensions, and money in retirement accounts. So don't empty your retirement accounts or sell off personal possessions to pay debts unless you're absolutely sure that you won't be filing bankruptcy.

Filing bankruptcy, needless to say, has it downsides, including the following:

✔ **It appears on your credit report for up to ten years.** As a result, you'll have difficulty obtaining credit, especially in the years immediately following your filing. (You may be able to obtain a secured credit card, which requires you to deposit money in a bank account equal to the credit limit on your credit card.) However, if you already have problems on your credit report (because of late payments or a failure to pay previous debts), the damage has already been done. And without savings, you're probably not going to be making major purchases (such as a home) in the next several years anyway.

✔ **It incurs significant court filing and legal fees.** These can easily exceed $1,000, especially in higher cost-of-living areas.

✔ **It can cause emotional stress.** Admitting that your personal income can't keep pace with your debt obligations is a painful thing to do. Although filing bankruptcy clears the decks of debt and gives you a fresh financial start, feeling a profound sense of failure (and sometimes shame) is common.

✔ **It becomes part of the public record.** Another part of the emotional side of filing bankruptcy is that you must open your personal financial affairs to court scrutiny and court control during the several months it takes to administer a bankruptcy. A court-appointed bankruptcy trustee oversees your case and tries to recover as much of your property as possible to satisfy the creditors — those to whom you owe money.

Deciphering the bankruptcy laws

If you want to have a leisurely afternoon read, then the bankruptcy laws are definitely not for you. I'm here to help clarify the two forms of personal bankruptcy in case you're considering taking this action:

✔ **Chapter 7:** Chapter 7 allows you to discharge or cancel certain debts. This form of bankruptcy makes the most sense when you have significant debts that you're legally allowed to cancel.

✔ **Chapter 13:** Chapter 13 comes up with a repayment schedule that requires you to pay your debts over several years. Chapter 13 stays on your credit record (just like Chapter 7), but it doesn't eliminate debt, so its value is limited — usually to dealing with debts like taxes that can't be discharged through bankruptcy. Chapter 13 can keep creditors at bay until a repayment schedule is worked out in the courts.

The Bankruptcy Abuse and Prevention Act of 2005 contains the elements of personal bankruptcy laws now in effect, which include the following:

✔ **Required counseling:** Before filing for bankruptcy, individuals are mandated to complete credit counseling, the purpose of which is to explore your options for dealing with debt, including (but not limited to) bankruptcy and developing a debt repayment plan.

To actually have debts discharged through bankruptcy, the law requires a second type of counseling called "debtor education." All credit counseling and debtor education must be completed by an approved organization on the U.S. Trustee's Web site (www.usdoj.gov/ust). Click the link "Credit Counseling & Debtor Education."

✔ **Means testing:** Some high-income earners are precluded from filing the form of bankruptcy that actually discharges debts (Chapter 7 bankruptcy) and instead are forced to use the form of bankruptcy that involves a repayment plan (Chapter 13 bankruptcy). The law does allow for differences in income by making adjustments based on your state of residence and family size. The expense side of the equation is considered as well, and allowances are determined by county and metropolitan area. For more information, click the "Means Testing Information" link on the U.S. Trustee's Web site (www. usdoj.gov/ust).

✔ **Rules to prevent people from moving to take advantage of a more-lenient state's bankruptcy laws:** Individual states have their own provisions for how much personal property and home equity you can keep. Prior to the passage of the 2005 laws, in some cases, soon before filing bankruptcy, people actually moved to a state that allowed them to keep more. Under the new law, you must live in a state for at least two years before filing bankruptcy in that state and using that state's personal property exemptions. To use a given state's homestead exemption, which dictates how much home equity you may protect, you must have lived in that state for at least 40 months.

Obtaining sound bankruptcy advice

No one should rush into filing bankruptcy. But you also don't want to make the mistake of not considering the option if your debt has become overwhelming. If you've seriously investigated bankruptcy and want more information than I provide in this chapter, I suggest that you check out the book *The New Bankruptcy: Will It Work for You?* (Nolo Press), by attorney Stephen Elias.

If you're comfortable with your decision to file and you think that you can complete the paperwork, you may be able to do it yourself. The book *How to File for Chapter 7 Bankruptcy* (Nolo Press), by attorneys Elias, Albin Renauer, and Robin Leonard, comes with all the necessary filing forms.

Preventing Consumer Debt Relapses

Regardless of how you deal with paying off your debt, you're at risk of re-accumulating debt if you've run up debt in the past. The following list highlights tactics you can use to limit the influence credit cards and consumer debt hold over your life:

- ✔ **Replace your credit card with a debit card.** See the section "Discovering debit cards: Convenience without credit temptation" earlier in this chapter for the details.

- ✔ **Think in terms of total cost.** Everything sounds cheaper in terms of monthly payments — that's how salespeople entice you into buying things you can't afford. Take a calculator along, if necessary, to tally up the sticker price, interest charges, and upkeep. The total cost will scare you. It should.

- ✔ **Stop the junk mail avalanche.** Look at your daily mail — I bet half of it is solicitations and mail-order catalogs. You can save some trees and time sorting junk mail by removing yourself from most mailing lists. To remove your name from mailing lists, register through the Web site www.dmachoice.org/dma/member/home.action.

  To remove your name from the major credit reporting agency lists that are used by credit card solicitation companies, call 888-567-8688. Also, tell credit card companies you have cards with that you want your account marked to indicate that you don't want your personal information shared with telemarketing firms.

- ✔ **Go shopping with a small amount of cash and no plastic or checks.** That way, you can spend only what little cash you have with you!

- ✔ **Identify and treat spending addictions.** Some people become addicted to spending and it becomes a chronic problem that can interfere with other aspects of their lives.

Check out Debtors Anonymous (DA), a nonprofit organization that provides support, primarily through group meetings. To find a DA support group in your area, visit the organization's Web site at www.debtorsanonymous.org or contact its headquarters at 781-453-2743.

Part II
Grown-up Stuff

The 5th Wave   By Rich Tennant

"Can you explain your mortgage program again, this time without using the phrase 'yada, yada, yada'?"

In this part . . .

*I*f you want to buy a home, you're probably going to need to borrow money. When you borrow money, you need to understand and maximize your credit score, a topic I cover in this part. I also devote a chapter to housing, in which I discuss your various options, including renting. Finally, I discuss the sometimes prickly topic of relationships and money.

Chapter 6

Everything Credit: Scores and Reports

● ●

In This Chapter

▶ Understanding your credit reports and credit scores

▶ Obtaining your credit reports and credit scores

▶ Improving your credit score

▶ Protecting yourself from identity theft

● ●

*Y*ou may not have given much thought to your credit report and may not know what your current credit score is. If you find yourself in that boat, I want you to pay special attention to this chapter. You should care about your credit report and credit score because lenders universally use credit scores to predict the likelihood that you'll repay a loan, and they won't agree to offer you a loan without first examining your credit details. If you already have a good grasp of your credit report and credit score, congratulations. You're on the right track, but I hope to show you some additional steps you can take to help your situation.

In this chapter, I explain the difference between your credit report and credit score and how to improve the two. I also detail how lenders and others use your credit information. Finally, I explain how to keep from falling victim to identity theft, which can damage your credit reports and scores and cost you time and money.

The Lowdown on Credit Reports and Credit Scores

Your credit report and credit score play a vital role in your financial well-being. Therefore, you want to use them to your advantage. The following sections define credit reports and scores, explain how credit bureaus come up with them, point out how lenders use this information, and discuss how you can get your credit going when you're in your 20s.

Differentiating between credit reports and credit scores

Credit reports and credit scores are different from each other, and you should understand upfront what they are and aren't. The following spells out their characteristics in greater detail.

Credit reports

Your personal *credit reports* are a compilation and history (assembled by credit bureaus such as Equifax, Experian, and TransUnion) of your various credit accounts.

Your credit report details when each account was opened, the latest balance, your payment history, and so on. It specifies your track record of making payments in a timely or late fashion (including bankruptcies) and whether you've failed to pay off previous debts. Your credit report also shows who has made inquiries on your report when you've applied for credit.

Credit scores

Your *credit score* is a three-digit score based on information in your personal credit report. Because each of three credit bureaus issues its own report, you actually have three different (although typically similar) credit scores.

FICO is the leading credit score in the industry and was developed by Fair, Isaac and Company. FICO scores range from a low of 300 to a high of 850. Most scores fall in the 600s and 700s, with the median around 720. As with college entrance examinations such as the SAT, higher scores are better. (In recent years, the major credit bureaus have developed their own credit-scoring systems, but most lenders still predominantly use FICO.) You generally qualify for the best lending rates if your credit score is in the mid-700s or higher.

The higher your credit score, the lower your predicted likelihood of defaulting on a loan. Conversely, consumers with low credit scores have dramatically higher rates of falling behind on their loans. Thus, low credit scorers are considered much riskier borrowers, and fewer lenders are willing to offer them a given loan; those who do so charge relatively high rates.

Understanding how credit scores are determined

You have many credit scores, not just one. The reason you have multiple scores is because each of the three major credit bureau reports has somewhat different information about you and generates a unique score. But most consumers find, not surprisingly, that their three FICO scores are fairly similar.

Credit scores change over time as your credit reports change. If you have a low score, the potential for change is good news because you can improve your score, perhaps significantly, in the weeks, months, and years ahead. The bureaus weigh current behavior more heavily than past behavior, though increasing your score is harder to do than decreasing it.

To have a credit score, you need to use credit. The FICO scoring system requires you to have at least one account open for a minimum of six months on your credit report and one account that has been updated in the most recent six months (it can be the same account).

The factors that determine your credit score include

- **Your payment history:** Your record of paying bills determines about 35 percent of your credit score.

    Your score decreases with a recent negative mark (a late payment, for example), with a high frequency of negative marks, and with the severity of the negative mark (for instance, a 60-day late payment is worse than a 30-day late payment).

✔ **How much you owe:** This factor, which accounts for 30 percent of your score, examines the total amount that you owe, as well as the amount by type of loan. The more you owe relative to your credit limits, the more adverse the effect on your credit score (most Americans use less than 30 percent of their available credit). With revolving debt (credit cards, credit lines), the greater the gap between your balances and your credit limits, the better. Also, paying down installment loans (mortgages, auto loans) relative to the amount you originally borrowed will boost your credit score.

✔ **How long you've had credit:** Generally speaking, the longer you've had credit, the better for your credit score. This factor, which comprises 15 percent of your score, considers the average age of your accounts as well as the age of your oldest account.

✔ **Your last application for credit:** Applying for and opening new accounts, especially multiple new accounts, can reduce your credit score. This factor accounts for 10 percent of your FICO score.

✔ **The types of credit you use:** The FICO score rewards you for having a "healthy mix" of different types of credit (such as a mortgage, credit cards, and so on), although FICO is vague about what the best mix is. This factor accounts for 10 percent of your credit score.

Knowing the value of a good credit score

Generally, the higher your credit score, the better the loan terms (especially the interest rate) you receive and the more likely your loan applications are approved.

Over the course of your adult life, having a high credit score can save you tens (and perhaps hundreds) of thousands of dollars. Additionally, you can earn more money by being able to borrow money to make investments, such as in real estate or a small business.

Lenders aren't the only ones that use credit scores. The following individuals also use credit scores:

✔ **Landlords:** A high credit score can lead to the approval of your apartment rental application.

✔ **Insurance agents:** A high credit score can help you pay lower rates on certain types of insurance.

✔ **Prospective employers:** Significant problems on your credit report can cause some employers to turn you down for a job.

Jump-starting your credit score

If you're just starting out financially, you may not have a credit score yet, simply because you don't have enough information on your credit report. Don't despair. To obtain a credit score if you don't yet have credit, the following actions help:

✔ **Establish a checking and savings account (and even a debit card).** Doing so demonstrates financial responsibility and stability.

✔ **Get added to someone's credit card as a joint or authorized user.** Make sure that this person is very responsible and shares your goal of keeping a terrific credit report and score.

✔ **Have someone with good credit cosign a loan with you.** I would only advise doing this with a relative, and only if the two of you have a long discussion about what could go wrong and have an agreement in writing to minimize the potential for misunderstandings.

✔ **Apply for a credit card in college because approval is relatively easy.**
Just be sure to get a card with a low annual rate and no or a low annual fee. And be careful not to rack up balances you can't immediately pay off every month.

✔ **If you can't get a regular credit card, apply for a department store or gas charge card.** Doing so is generally easier, but watch out for high interest rates and other fees if you can't pay your bill in full each month.

✔ **Apply for a secured credit card.** This type of card requires that you keep money on deposit in the bank that issues the card.

Getting Your Hands on Your Credit Reports and Scores

Given the importance of your personal credit report, you may be pleased to know that you're entitled to receive a free copy of your credit report annually from each of the three credit bureaus (Equifax, Experian, and TransUnion).

If you visit www.annualcreditreport.com, you can view and print copies of your credit report information from each of the three credit agencies (alternatively, call 877-322-8228 and have your reports mailed to you). After entering some personal data at the Web site, check the box indicating that you want to obtain all three credit reports, as each report may have slightly different information. You'll then be directed to one of the three bureaus, and after you finish verifying that you are who you claim to be at that site, you can easily navigate back to www.annualcreditreport.com so you can continue to the next agency's site.

Your credit reports don't include your credit score because credit bureaus aren't required to include it by the federal law mandating that the three credit agencies provide a free credit report annually to each U.S. citizen who requests a copy. Thus, if you want to obtain your credit score, you need to pay for it. (One exception: You're entitled to the credit score used by a lender who denies your loan application.)

Although you can request your credit score from Fair, Isaac and Company, the charge is $15.95 per request, so it can cost you about $50 to see your FICO score from all three credit bureaus. Save your money by ordering your score from the individual credit bureaus when you obtain your credit report(s) through www.annualcreditreport.com. Experian (888-397-3742), for example, charges just $7.95 to obtain your current credit score. Call each credit bureau's toll-free phone number to buy your credit score instead of visiting the bureau's Web site, because finding the proper Web page to buy your score on a one-time basis without getting signed up for other, ongoing, far more costly services and monitoring is a nightmare. (Your local bank may offer you your credit score for free.)

If you do spring for your current credit score, be clear about what you're buying. You may not realize that you're agreeing to some sort of an ongoing credit-monitoring service for, say, $50 to $100+ per year. Furthermore, avoid services claiming to offer you free access to your credit score when in fact what you're signing up for is an ongoing credit-monitoring service that costs a lot over time.

Scrutinizing Your Credit Reports to Improve Them

Because your credit score is based on the information in your credit report, the first step to improving your score is to review each of your three reports. (The preceding section explains how to obtain these reports.) The following sections point out what you need to look for, what you can do to fix inaccurate information, and how you can improve your reports and credit score.

Identifying errors and getting them fixed

Carefully look through your credit reports for any potential inaccuracies. If you find any errors, you want to get them corrected quickly.

Follow these steps to ensure that you properly vet each report:

1. **Review the identifying information to be sure that other folks' information hasn't gotten mixed up with yours.**

   Look for the following errors:

   - Names that aren't yours
   - Incorrect Social Security numbers
   - Incorrect date of birth
   - Addresses where you haven't resided

2. **Inspect the credit accounts for problems, such as**

- Accounts that don't belong to you

- Negative entries that don't belong to you (such as late payments and *charge-offs,* which are amounts you supposedly borrowed that a lender no longer expects to get back from you)

- Negative entries that are more than seven years old

- Debts that your spouse incurred before marriage

- Incorrect entries due to identity theft or a credit bureau snafu that mixed up someone else's information with yours

3. **Examine the collection actions and public records section of your report for the following errors:**

- Bankruptcies more than ten years old or ones that aren't listed by a specific bankruptcy code chapter (such as a Chapter 7 bankruptcy)

- Lawsuits, judgments, or paid tax liens more than seven years old

- Paid liens or judgments that are listed as unpaid

- Loans that went into collection that are listed under more than one collection agency

- Any negative information that isn't yours

If you identify any errors, you can submit corrections by using one of the forms for disputing incorrect information that accompany your credit reports. All credit bureaus are mandated to investigate and correct errors within 30 days. Your persistence may be required.

Boosting your credit score

After you get your credit report cleaned up, here are some ways to improve your credit score:

✔ **Pay your bills on time.** The better your credit score, the more a late payment harms your score because such a change in behavior may indicate increasing financial difficulties.

To avoid making late payments, consider putting your bills on an automatic payment system. If you've never used automatic payments and you're skittish, try the system first with one company you trust the most. Another option is to put the charges on your credit card. Only do this, however, if you always pay your credit card bill in full each month. Be cautious charging large bills on your credit card because using a big portion of your available credit can reduce your credit score.

✔ **Pay down your debt.** Paying down your debts over time is exactly the kind of responsible credit behavior that lenders want to see in the folks to whom they lend money. The lower the portion your balances are of your credit limits (try to keep them under 30 percent), the better your credit score will be. For this reason, you should avoid both consolidating debts and charging so much on a card in a month that you near the card's credit limit.

✔ **Avoid closing credit card and other revolving accounts.** Closing accounts makes your remaining balances look that much larger in comparison to your total available credit. Also, closing older accounts lowers the average age of your credit accounts, which reduces your credit score.

✔ **Apply for credit sparingly.** Applying for credit too frequently lowers your credit score.

Preventing Identity Theft

A study by Javelin Strategy & Research found that folks ages 18 to 24 are at significantly greater risk for identity theft than people in other age groups. Therefore, you must be proactive in preventing your personal information and accounts (bank, investment, credit, and debit) from being used by crooks to commit identity theft and fraud.

Victims of identity theft can suffer trashed credit reports, reduced ability to qualify for loans and even jobs (with employers who check credit reports), out-of-pocket costs, and dozens of hours of time to clean up the mess and clean their credit records and name.

According to the aforementioned study, people in their early 20s are at greater risk for identity theft because

✔ **Their use of social networking exposes confidential information.** Younger people use social networking Web sites more heavily than others, and these sites promote the sharing of personal information. Those who use social networking sites are twice as likely to suffer identity theft problems.

✔ **They're common targets of friendly fraud.** Younger people are at far greater risk of *friendly fraud,* in which the perpetrator (family members, domestic workers, employees who have access to personal information, and so on) is known to the victim.

✔ **They take much longer than older folks to detect fraud.** Younger people are less likely to closely monitor accounts and credit reports that could reveal that fraud is taking place.

Here's how to greatly reduce your chances of falling victim to identity theft:

✔ **Don't provide personal information over the phone, unless you initiated the call and you know well the company or person on the other end of the line.** And don't fall for incoming calls that your caller ID says are coming from a particular business because folks have found ways to dupe caller ID systems.

✔ **Ignore e-mails soliciting personal information or action.** Online crooks are clever and can generate a return/ sender e-mail address that looks like it comes from a known institution but really does not. This unscrupulous practice is known as *phishing,* and if you bite the bait, visit the site, and provide the requested personal information, your reward is likely to be some sort of future identity theft problem. Never click on links in e-mails, and only access your online accounts by typing in your bank's URL or by using your own created bookmarks.

✔ **Review your monthly financial statements.** Although your bank, mutual fund, and investment company may call you if they notice unusual activity on one of your accounts, some people discover problematic account activity by simply reviewing their monthly credit card, checking account, and other statements. Review line items on your statement to be sure that all the transactions are yours.

You can simplify this process by closing unnecessary accounts. The more credit cards and credit lines you have, the more likely you are to have problems with identity theft and to overspend and carry debt balances. Unless you maintain a card for small business transactions, you really *need* only one piece of plastic with a Visa or MasterCard logo. Give preference to a debit card if you have a history of accumulating credit card debt balances.

✔ **Periodically review your credit reports.** Some identity theft victims have found out about credit accounts opened in their name by reviewing their credit reports. Because you're entitled to a free credit report from each of the three major credit agencies every year, I recommend reviewing one agency report every four months, which enables you to keep a close eye on your reports and still obtain them without cost. Refer to the earlier section "Scrutinizing Your Credit Reports to Improve Them" for more information.

✔ **Freeze your credit reports.** Many states enable consumers, typically for a nominal fee, to *freeze* their credit information. Doing so puts you in total control of who may access your credit report. (But freezing also means that you have to give permission every time someone wants to examine your credit report, unless you place a temporary thaw on the account.) For an up-to-date listing of state freeze laws, visit the Web site `www.pirg.org/consumer/credit/statelaws.htm`.

✔ **Avoid placing personal information on checks.** Information that's useful to identity thieves and that you shouldn't put on your checks includes your credit card number, driver's license number, Social Security number, and so on. I also encourage you to leave your home address off your preprinted checks when you order them. Otherwise, everyone whose hands your check passes through gets free access to that information.

When writing a check to a merchant, question the need for adding personal information to the check (in fact, in numerous states, it's against the law to request and place credit card numbers on checks). Use a debit card instead for such transactions.

✔ **Protect your computer.** If you keep personal and financial data on your computer, use up-to-date virus protection software and a firewall, and password-protect access to your programs and files.

✔ **Protect your snail mail.** Stealing mail is pretty easy, especially if your mail is delivered to a curbside box. Consider using a locked mailbox or a post office box to protect your incoming mail from theft. Consider having your investment and other important statements sent to you via e-mail, or simply access them online and eliminate mail delivery of the paper copies. Minimize your outgoing mail and save yourself hassles by signing up for automatic bill payment for as many bills as you can. Drop the rest of your outgoing mail in a secure U.S. postal box, such as those you find at the post office. (If you continue receiving paper statements, consider getting a shredder to shred documents you want to dispose of.)

My story of identity theft

I can speak from personal experience when it comes to identity theft. It happened to me in my late 20s when a crook withdrew money from my checking account by using personal information that was stolen from my wife's employer payroll department. This is but one of many ways you can fall victim to identity theft. In other cases, the criminal activity may develop with someone opening an account (such as a credit card) using someone's stolen personal information.

Chapter 7

Housing: Comparing Renting and Buying

· ·

In This Chapter

▶ Comparing the advantages and disadvantages of renting versus owning

▶ Assessing your finances before buying a home

▶ Searching for the right house for you

▶ Hiring a real estate agent

▶ Considering your mortgage options

· ·

*O*ver the decades of your adult life, you need a place to live. Housing is important because you spend a lot of time in it, and its location affects your commuting to work and other activities. And you spend plenty of money on housing, whether you rent it or own it. Along with taxes, housing expenses are one of the top two expenses for most people.

This chapter explores your housing options and helps you understand the costs of buying and owning a home and compare that option to renting. If you decide to purchase a home, I walk you through the major elements of searching for and negotiating your best deal on a home for purchase.

The Ins and Outs of Renting

Most books on home buying and real estate fail to offer a balanced perspective of renting versus buying. Too many of them only extol the virtues of buying and owning property without discussing the drawbacks. In this section, I discuss the benefits and long-term costs of renting. I also cover the important details of rental applications and contracts.

Seeing the benefits of renting

Although owning a home and investing in real estate generally pay off well over the long term, renting has its advantages. Some of the financially successful renters I've met include people who pay low rent, either because they live in small housing and/or have roommates, or they live in a rent-controlled building. If you can consistently save 10 percent or more of your earnings, which you may be able to do through a low-cost rental, you're probably on track to achieving your financial goals.

Renting has the following pros:

- **You can avoid worrying about or being responsible for fixing up the property.** Your landlord is responsible.

- **You have more financial and psychological flexibility.** You may not be sure that you'll stay with your current employer or chosen career, and you may change direction in the future and not want the financial overhead that comes with a mortgage. And if you want to move, you can generally do so a lot more easily as a renter than you can as a homeowner.

- **You can have all your money in financial assets that you can tap into more easily.** Some people enter their retirement years with a substantial portion of their wealth tied up in their home, a challenge that you don't face when renting over the long haul. Homeowners who have *equity* (the difference between the market value of the property and the debt owed on it) tied up in a home at retirement can downsize to a less-costly property to free up cash and/or take out a reverse mortgage on their home equity.

Considering the long-term costs of renting

When you crunch the numbers to find out what owning rather than renting a comparable place may cost you on a monthly basis, you may discover that owning isn't as expensive as you thought. Or you may find that owning costs more than renting. This discovery may tempt you to think that, financially speaking, renting is cheaper than owning.

Be careful not to jump to conclusions. Remember that you're looking at the cost of owning versus renting *today.* What about 10, 20, or 30 years from now? As an owner, your biggest monthly expense — the mortgage payment — doesn't increase, assuming that you have a fixed-rate mortgage (for an explanation of fixed-rate and other types of mortgages, see the "Understanding your mortgage options" section later in the chapter). Your property taxes, homeowners insurance, and maintenance expenses, which are generally far less than your mortgage payment, should only increase with the cost of living. And remember that as a homeowner you build equity in your property; that equity can be significant by your retirement.

When you rent, however, your entire monthly rent is subject to inflation. (Living in a *rent-controlled unit,* where the annual increase allowed in your rent is capped, is the exception to this rule.)

Completing your rental application

When you're in the market for a rental, you'll probably complete an application. You'll be asked to provide such information as your name, current address, date of birth, occupation, employer, banking information, credit history, current landlord and rental terms, and a couple of references.

Here are some tips to keep in mind as you're completing your rental application:

✔ **Put your best foot forward.** Just as a good résumé helps you interest an employer and land a job, your rental application helps you secure a place to live. So it's important to fill it out neatly and completely. Does that mean you need to list everything on it, including less than flattering information? As with your résumé, tell the truth but remember the advertising value of the document.

With regards to other sources of income, you're under no obligation to detail alimony, child support, or your spouse's annual income unless you want that information considered in your application.

✓ **Recognize that you're authorizing the release of personal and confidential information.** Rental applications generally have a section requiring your signature stating, "I authorize an investigation of my credit, tenant history, banking, and employment for the purposes of renting a house, apartment, or condominium from this owner, manager, brokerage, finder, agent, or leasing company."

✓ **Consider the length of the lease commitment.** Most landlords prefer tenants who are stable renters and who remain for long periods of time (years, not months). Especially if you may want to move to buy a place or relocate for a future job, having a one-year lease that goes month to month after the first year is a good compromise.

✓ **Rent where you might like to buy.** If you're getting close to wanting to buy your own home, try renting in the area you think you'd most like to buy. What better way to test out whether you'll actually enjoy living in an area?

Figuring the Costs of Owning and Making It Happen Financially

Buying a home can be financially rewarding, but owning a property is a big financial commitment that may backfire if you get in over your head or overpay.

In this section, I help you with comparing the costs of buying versus renting, determining what you can afford, figuring out how much to borrow, and accumulating the down payment.

Deciding to buy

Before you determine whether you want to actually buy a home, you want to figure out how long you plan on living in the home.

Financially speaking, you really shouldn't buy a home unless you anticipate being there for at least three to five years or more. Buying and selling a property entails a lot of expenses, including the cost of getting a mortgage (points; application and appraisal fees), inspection expenses, moving costs, real estate agents' commissions, and title insurance. To cover these transaction costs plus the additional costs of ownership, a property needs to appreciate about 15 percent during the tenure of your ownership.

If you need or want to move in a couple of years, counting on 15 percent appreciation is risky. If you're fortunate and you happen to buy before a sharp upturn in housing prices, you may get it. Otherwise, you'll lose money on the deal.

Comparing the costs of owning versus renting

Some people assume that owning costs more than renting, but owning doesn't have to cost a lot. Owning may even cost less than renting, especially with the opportunity to buy at lower prices thanks to the decline in home prices in the late 2000s in many parts of the country.

Buying seems a lot more expensive than renting if you compare your monthly rent (from hundreds of dollars to more than $1,000, depending on where you live) to a property's purchase price, which is usually a much larger number — perhaps $100,000 to $250,000. But you must compare the expenses the same way. When you consider a home purchase, you're forced to think about your housing expenses in one huge chunk rather than in a monthly rent check.

To make a fair comparison between ownership and rental costs, figure what it costs on a monthly basis to buy a place you desire versus what it costs to rent a comparable place. Remember that mortgage interest and property tax payments for your home are generally tax-deductible.

Considering your overall financial health

Before you buy a property and agree to a particular mortgage, take stock of your overall financial health (especially where you stand in terms of retirement planning). Don't trust a lender when he tells you what you can "afford" according to some formulas the bank uses to figure out what kind of a credit risk you are.

To determine how much a potential home buyer can borrow, lenders look primarily at annual income; they pay no attention to some major aspects of a borrower's overall financial situation. Even if you don't have money tucked away in retirement savings, or you have several children to clothe, feed, and help put through college, you still qualify for the same size loan as other people with the same income (assuming equal outstanding debts).

Calculating how much you can borrow

One general rule says that you can borrow up to about three times your annual income when buying a home. But, the maximum that a mortgage lender will loan you depends on interest rates. If rates fall, the monthly payment on a mortgage also drops. Thus, lower interest rates make real estate more affordable.

To determine how much they're willing to lend you, lenders start by totaling up your monthly housing expenses for a given home. They define your housing costs as

> mortgage payment + property taxes + homeowners insurance

Lenders typically loan you up to about 35 percent of your monthly gross (before taxes) income for the housing expense. (If you're self-employed, take your net income from the bottom line of your federal tax form Schedule C and divide by 12 to get your monthly gross income.)

Lenders also consider your other debts when deciding how much to lend you. These debts diminish the funds available to pay your housing expenses. Lenders add the amount you need to pay down on your other consumer debts (such as auto loans and credit cards) to your monthly housing expense. The total monthly costs of these debt payments plus your housing costs typically can't exceed 40 percent.

Accumulating your down payment

You generally qualify for the most favorable mortgage terms by making a down payment of at least 20 percent of the property's purchase price. In addition to saving money on interest, you can avoid the added cost of *private mortgage insurance (PMI)* by putting down this much. To protect against their losing money in the event you default on your loan, lenders usually require PMI, which costs several hundred dollars per year on a typical mortgage. (PMI compensates the lender in the event that it has to take over the property and the property ends up being worth less than the outstanding mortgage on it.)

Many folks, especially folks in their 20s, don't have enough cash on hand to make a 20 percent down payment on a home to avoid paying PMI. Here are a number of solutions for coming up with that 20 percent faster or for buying with less money down:

- ✔ **Minimize your spending.** See Chapter 4 for ideas.

- ✔ **Consider lower-priced properties.** Smaller properties and ones that need some work can help keep down the purchase price and, therefore, the required down payment.

- ✔ **Find financial partners.** Draft a legal contract to specify what happens if a partner wants out, divorces, or passes away.

- ✔ **Seek reduced down-payment financing.** Some property owners or developers may be willing to finance your purchase with 10 percent down, although you can't be as picky about properties because not as many are available under these terms — many need work or haven't been sold yet for other reasons.

✔ **Get family assistance.** If your parents, grandparents, or other relatives have money dozing away in a savings or CD account, they may be willing to lend (or even give) you the down payment.

For more home-buying strategies, get a copy of the latest edition of *Home Buying For Dummies* (Wiley), which I coauthored with real estate guru Ray Brown.

Finding the Right Property

In your search for a property to purchase, you have many options in today's real estate market. To find the right property for you, consider your choices:

✔ **Single-family home:** Some people's image of a home is a single-family house, perhaps with a lawn and a white picket fence. From an investment perspective, single-family homes generally do best in the long run. Most people, when they can afford it, prefer a stand-alone home.

✔ **Higher-density housing:** In some areas, particularly in higher-cost neighborhoods, you find the following choices:

• **Condominiums:** You own the unit and a share of everything else.

• **Town homes:** These properties are attached or row houses.

• **Cooperatives:** You own a share of the entire building.

The appeal of such higher-density housing is that it's generally less expensive. In some cases, you don't have to worry about some of the general maintenance because the homeowners association (which you pay for, directly or indirectly) takes care of it.

If you don't have the time, energy, or desire to keep up a property, shared/higher-density housing may make sense for you. You generally get more living space for your dollar, and it may also provide you with more security than a stand-alone home. However, shared housing is easier to build and hence easier to overbuild.

With that being said, you should remember that a rising tide raises all boats. In a good real estate market, all types of housing appreciate, although single-family homes tend to do best. Shared-housing values tend to increase the most in densely populated urban areas with little available land for new building.

From an investment-return perspective, if you can afford a smaller single-family home rather than a larger shared-housing unit, buy the single-family home. Be especially wary of buying shared housing in suburban areas with lots of developable land.

Here are some additional tips to keep in mind to help you find the best property for your situation and to buy a home most likely to increase in value:

✔ **Cast a broad net and look at different types of properties in a number of communities before you narrow your search.** Be open-minded, and figure out which of your many criteria for a home you really care about.

✔ **Even (and especially) if you fall in love with a house, go back to the neighborhood at various times of the day and on different days of the week.** Travel to and from your prospective new home during commute hours to see how long your commute will really take. Knock on a few doors and meet your potential neighbors. You may discover, for example, that a flock of chickens lives in the backyard next door or that the street and basement frequently flood.

✔ **Examine the area schools.** Go visit them. Don't rely on statistics about test scores. Talk to parents and teachers. What's really going on at the school? Even if you don't have kids, the quality of the local school has a direct bearing on the property's value.

✔ **Determine whether crime is a problem.** Call the local police department. Will future development be allowed? If so, what type?

Neighborhood Scout (www.neighborhoodscout.com) is a useful Web site for this kind of data and more.

✔ **Talk to the planning department.** What are your property taxes going to be?

✔ **Identify any other potential risks.** Is the property located in an area susceptible to major risks, such as floods, mudslides, fires, or earthquakes?

Consider these issues even if they're not important to you, because they can affect the property's resale value. Make sure that you know what you're getting yourself into before you buy.

Working with Real Estate Agents

A top-notch real estate agent can be a significant help when you purchase or sell a property. But because they work on commission and get paid a percentage of the sale price, real estate agents face numerous conflicts of interest. So don't expect an agent to give you objective advice about what you should do given your overall financial situation. Examine your financial situation before you decide to begin working with an agent.

Interview several agents and check references. Ask agents for the names and phone numbers of at least three clients they worked with in the past six months (in the geographical area in which you're looking). For more advice on hiring a good agent, see Chapter 17.

Financing Your Home

A mortgage loan from a bank or other source makes up the difference between the cash you intend to put into the purchase and the agreed-upon selling price of the real estate. This section reviews the different options you have for financing your home, explains which ones are best, and discusses how to get your loan approved.

Understanding your mortgage options

Three major types of mortgages exist — those with a fixed interest rate, those with a variable or adjustable rate, and those that are a combination of the two.

✔ **Fixed-rate mortgages:** These are usually issued for a 15- or 30-year period and have interest rates that don't change. Because the interest rate stays the same, your monthly mortgage payment amount doesn't change. With a fixed-rate mortgage, you have no uncertainty or interest rate worries.

✔ **Adjustable-rate mortgage (ARM):** In contrast to a fixed-rate mortgage, an adjustable-rate mortgage (ARM) carries an interest rate that varies over time. Thus, the size of your monthly payment fluctuates. Because a mortgage payment makes an unusually large dent in most homeowners' checkbooks anyway, signing up for an ARM without understanding its risks is dangerous.

So why would anyone want an ARM? Because of potential interest-rate savings, especially during the first few years of an adjustable loan, when the interest rate is typically lower than it is on a comparable fixed-rate loan.

✔ **Hybrid mortgage:** This type of mortgage combines features of both the fixed- and adjustable-rate mortgages. For example, the initial rate may hold constant for three to five years and then adjust once a year or every six months thereafter.

Deciding which mortgage type is best for you

You should weigh the pros and cons of each mortgage type and consider these issues to determine whether a fixed or adjustable mortgage is best for you. Think about the following questions to make that determination:

✔ **How much risk can you handle with the size of your monthly mortgage payment?** You can't afford much risk, for example, if your job and income are unstable and you need to borrow a lot or you have little slack in your monthly budget. If you're in this situation, stick with a fixed-rate loan. If interest rates rise, how can you afford the monthly payments — much less all the other expenses of home ownership? And don't forget to factor in reasonably predictable future expenses that may affect your ability to make payments. For example, are you planning to start a family soon? If so, your income may fall while your expenses rise (as they surely will).

If you can't afford the highest allowed payment on an adjustable-rate mortgage, don't take it. You shouldn't accept the chance that the interest rate may not rise that high — it might, and then you could lose your home! Ask your lender to calculate the highest possible maximum monthly payment on your loan. That's the payment you'd face if the interest rate on your loan were to go to the highest level allowed (the *lifetime cap*).

✔ **How long do you plan to keep the mortgage?** The savings on most adjustables is usually guaranteed in the first two or three years, because an adjustable-rate mortgage starts at a lower interest rate than a fixed one. If rates rise, you can end up giving back or losing the savings you achieve in the early years of the mortgage. In most cases, if you aren't going to keep your mortgage more than five to seven years, you're probably paying unnecessary interest costs to carry a fixed-rate mortgage.

You may want to look into a hybrid loan. These loans may make sense for you if you foresee a high probability of keeping your loan seven to ten years or less but want some stability in your monthly payments. The longer the initial rate stays locked in, the higher the rate.

Get a written itemization of charges from all lenders you're seriously considering so that you can more readily compare different lenders' mortgages and so you have no surprises when you close on your loan. And to minimize your chances of throwing money away on a loan for which you may not qualify, ask the lender whether you may not be approved for some reason. Be sure to disclose any problems you're aware of that are on your credit report or with the property.

Some lenders offer loans without *points* (upfront interest) or other lender charges. Remember: If lenders don't charge points or other fees, they have to make up the difference by charging a higher interest rate on your loan. Consider such loans only if you lack cash for closing or if you're planning to use the loan for just a few years.

Avoiding negative amortization and interest-only loans

As you make mortgage payments over time, the loan balance you still owe is gradually reduced, a process known as *amortizing* the loan. The reverse of this process — increasing your loan balance — is called *negative amortization*. You want to steer clear of negative-amortization mortgages.

Some ARMs allow negative amortization. Your outstanding loan balance can grow even though you're continuing to make mortgage payments when your mortgage payment is less than it really should be.

Taking on negative amortization is like paying only the minimum payment required on a credit card bill. You keep racking up greater interest charges on the balance as long as you make only the artificially low payment. Doing so defeats the whole purpose of borrowing an amount that fits your overall financial goals. And you may never get your mortgage paid off! Even worse, the increased interest you start to accrue on the unpaid interest added to your mortgage balance may not be tax-deductible because it doesn't qualify as interest incurred as part of the original purchase (what the IRS calls the *acquisition debt*).

The only way to know for certain whether a loan includes negative amortization is to ask. Some lenders aren't forthcoming about telling you. You find negative amortization more frequently on loans that lenders consider risky. If you're having trouble finding lenders who are willing to deal with your financial situation, be especially careful.

Some loans cap the increase of your monthly payment but not of the interest rate. The size of your mortgage payment may not reflect all the interest you owe on your loan. So rather than paying off the interest and some of your loan balance (or *principal*) every month, you're paying off some, but not all, of the interest you owe. Thus, the extra unpaid interest you still owe is added to your outstanding debt.

Also tread carefully with *interest-only mortgages,* which are loans in which you pay only interest in the beginning years. Don't consider interest-only loans if you're stretching to be able to afford a home, and consider one only if you understand how they work and can afford the inevitable jump in payments.

Getting your mortgage approved

When you're under contract to buy a property, having your loan denied after waiting several weeks can mean that you lose the property as well as the money you spent applying for the loan and having the property inspected. Some property sellers may be willing to give you an extension, but others won't. So you want to make sure that you get your mortgage approved.

Here's how to increase your chances of having your mortgage approved:

- ✔ **Get your finances in shape before you shop.** You won't know what you can afford to spend on a home until you whip your personal finances into shape. Do so before you begin to make offers on properties. This book can help you. If you have consumer debt, pay it down.

- ✔ **Clean up credit-report problems.** If you think you may have errors on your credit report, get a copy before you apply for a mortgage. Chapter 6 details how to obtain a free copy of your credit report and correct mistakes.

- ✔ **Get prequalified or preapproved.** When you get *prequalified,* a lender speaks with you about your financial situation and then calculates the maximum amount it's willing to lend you. *Preapproval* is much more in-depth and includes a lender's review of your financial statements. Just be sure not to waste your time and money getting preapproved if you're not really ready to get serious about buying.

- ✔ **Be upfront about problems.** You may be able to stop potential loan rejection by disclosing to your lender anything that may cause a problem before you apply.

✔ **Work around low/unstable income.** When you've been changing jobs or you're self-employed, your income may be down or unstable. Making a larger down payment is one way around this problem. You may try getting a cosigner, such as a relative. Be sure to have a written agreement, including who's responsible for payments.

✔ **Consider a backup loan.** You certainly should shop among different lenders, and you may want to apply to more than one for a mortgage. Disclose to each lender what you're doing; the second lender that pulls your credit report will see that another lender has already done so.

Putting Your Deal Together

After you do your homework on your personal finances, decide which kind of mortgage to choose, and research neighborhoods and home prices, you'll hopefully be ready to close in on your goal. Eventually, you'll find a home you want to buy. Before you make that first offer, though, you need to understand the importance of negotiations, inspections, and the other elements of a real estate deal:

✔ **Never fall in love with a property.** If you have money to burn and can't imagine life without the home you just discovered, pay what you will. Otherwise, remind yourself that other good properties are out there. Having a backup property in mind can help.

✔ **Find out about the property and owner before you make your offer.** How long has the property been on the market? What are its flaws? Why is the owner selling? The more you understand about the property and the seller's motivations, the better able you'll be to draft an offer that meets both parties' needs.

✔ **Get comparable sales data to support your price.** Pointing to recent and comparable home sales to justify your offer price strengthens your case.

✔ **Remember that price is only one of several negotiable items.** You may be able to get a seller to pay for certain repairs or improvements, to pay some of your closing costs, or to offer you favorable loan terms. Likewise, the real estate agent's commission is negotiable.

✔ **Spend the time and money to locate and hire good inspectors and other experts to evaluate the major systems and potential problem areas of the home.** When problems that you weren't aware of are uncovered, the inspection reports give you the information you need to go back and ask the property seller to fix the problems or reduce the property's purchase price to compensate you for correcting the deficiencies yourself.

✔ **Shop around for title insurance and escrow services.** Mortgage lenders require *title insurance* to protect against someone else claiming legal title to your property. *Escrow charges* pay for neutral third-party services to ensure that the instructions of the purchase contract or refinance are fulfilled and that everyone gets paid. Many people don't seem to understand that title insurance and escrow fees vary from company to company. When you call around for title insurance and escrow fee quotes, make sure that you understand all the fees. Many companies tack on all sorts of charges for things such as courier fees and express mail. If you find a company with lower prices and want to use it, ask for an itemization in writing so that you don't have any surprises.

Chapter 8

Relationships and Money

● ●

In This Chapter

▶ Managing financial considerations with roommates

▶ Understanding unique aspects of living together

▶ Maintaining financial harmony in a marriage

● ●

*S*omeday you may plan on getting married. Before that day, you'll likely live together with other people. Perhaps you'll simply have roommates, or you may live with your significant other and not yet be married.

When you live with others, you may share household expenses and other matters. In this chapter, I discuss how best to handle the financial side of having roommates, having romantic partners, or being married.

Handling Roommates

As I discuss in Chapter 4, sharing the rent with roommates is a time-tested way of containing your housing costs when you're young, single, and need housing. However, having roommates doesn't mean that you're free of problems. In fact, how you handle living with roommates can potentially have significant effects on your own personal finances.

If you're going to share a rental with roommates, a wise decision is to draft a roommate agreement and have all your rental mates sign it. A *roommate agreement* basically is a legal agreement of important issues between you and your roommate(s). The following are some characteristics of a standard roommate agreement:

✔ The agreement's financial terms are legally enforceable with your roommates, but they aren't legally binding with your landlord.

✔ To keep legal fees down, the agreement should include a mediation clause.

✔ The agreement should reflect your concerns and priorities. For example, if you need your eight hours of sleep every night, and you therefore require peace and quiet starting at 10 p.m., then the agreement should spell out those sorts of details. Examples of items you may want to cover in the agreement include

- Who pays how much rent, when, and to whom

- How bedrooms are allocated and whether rent depends on which one you have

- Who's responsible for which chores

- How parking is handled if it's limited

- Whether pets and overnight guests are allowed

- How much notice should be given when someone needs to move out

- Whose responsibility it is to find a replacement roommate

If one of your roommates does something in violation of the rental agreement, you all are responsible. Suppose, for example, that one of your roommates fails to pay the rent on time, damages the rental unit in some way, or has loud parties that warrant calls to the police by neighbors. You and your roommates are all responsible for the missing rent, the damages, or the intrusion on your neighbors. The landlord can also add insult to injury and terminate your rental contract. (One exception to this is if you as a renter have subleased to a tenant and that's the person who has violated the rules of the rental agreement. Another related exception is if your rental is subject to local rental control laws and you're designated as a master tenant with authority to approve and evict tenants.)

Some landlords make an effort to identify the bad apple in an otherwise good group of tenants and may not hold the good apples responsible.

Living-Together Contracts

What if you're involved in a relationship with someone and you're living with that person? That situation may be more complicated than having a roommate and dealing with a contract for a roommate because your finances and personal possessions may be more intertwined. You may want to consider a *living-together contract,* which is used by folks who aren't married to each other.

Practically speaking, your agreement can help you avoid trouble when you mix your money and property, and it can make clear your intentions and expectations regarding property ownership, household expenses, and the like. It can also greatly ease the division or distribution of property after a breakup or death. On a more personal note, the process of negotiating and drafting your agreement may well strengthen your abilities to communicate with and understand each other.

Here's an overview of the legal rules and practical concerns you should think about before drafting a contract of your own. Nearly all states recognize and enforce contracts between unmarried partners. Topics you may want to address in your contract include

- ✔ **Personal property:** You may want to delineate and keep separate any property that you owned before moving in together, as well as property you inherit or receive as a gift. If you want to divide ownership of property purchased during the period of living together some other way than 50-50, specify that.

- ✔ **Living expenses:** Your agreement should specify how your household's expenses are divvied up. You can discuss pooling your money versus keeping separate accounts, as well as sharing expenses equally or through some other method.

- ✔ **Parting ways:** Your agreement should detail how your property, especially jointly owned property, is divided in the event one of you decides to move out.

- ✔ **Death:** Your agreement (in addition to your will; check out the later sidebar "Preparing wills and other important legal documents" for more information) should also detail what happens to each person's property should one or both of you die.

✔ **Dispute resolution:** Providing for mediation and/or arbitration is a time-tested way to effectively resolve disputes.

Getting Married

To help ensure a happy marriage, couples should discuss a plethora of issues before getting hitched. Money matters are certainly on that short list. Unfortunately, money issues are also on the list of frequently neglected and avoided topics for engaged couples. Not surprisingly, money issues are one of the leading causes of marital discord and divorce. Discussing money with a loved one makes most people uncomfortable, and in many families, talking about money is a taboo topic.

Merging your financial decisions and resources doesn't have to be unpleasant and a source of stress. Even if you're largely in agreement about your financial goals and strategies, managing as two is far different from managing as one. Here are my tips to prepare for marriage:

✔ **Talk money before getting married.** Many couples never talk about their financial and personal goals and expectations before marriage, and failing to do so breaks up way too many marriages. Finances are just one of the many issues you need to discuss. Ensuring that you know what you're getting yourself into is a good way to minimize your chances for heartache. In addition to discussing the topics in the rest of this list, also discuss your feelings and goals pertaining to earning, spending, saving, and investing money. Ministers, priests, and rabbis sometimes offer premarital counseling to help bring issues and differences to the surface.

✔ **Discuss merging finances versus maintaining separate accounts.** I generally prefer that couples merge their finances. Marriage is a partnership, and you're supposed to be on the same team. In some marriages, however, spouses may choose to keep some money separate so that they don't feel their spouse's scrutiny with regard to different spending preferences. Spouses who've been through divorce may choose to keep the assets they bring into the new marriage separate in order to protect their money in the event of another divorce. As long as you're jointly accomplishing what you need to financially, some separation of money is okay. But for the health of your marriage, don't hide money from each other, and if you're the higher-income spouse, don't assume power and control over your joint income.

✓ **Understand and optimize your employer benefits.** If one or both of you have access to a package of employee benefits through an employer, determine how best to make use of those benefits. Coordinating and using the best that each package has to offer is like getting a pay raise. If you both have access to health insurance, compare which of you has better benefits. Likewise, one of you may have a better retirement savings plan — one that matches and offers superior investment options. Unless you can afford to save the maximum through both your plans, saving more in the better plan increases your combined assets. (Note: If you're concerned about what will happen if you save more in one of your retirement plans and then you divorce, in most states, the money is considered part of your joint assets to be divided equally.)

✓ **Discuss life and disability insurance needs.** If you and your spouse can make do without each other's income, you may not need any income-protecting insurance. However, if, like many husbands and wives, you both depend on each other's incomes, or if one of you depends fully or partly on the other's income, you may each need long-term disability and term life insurance policies (see Chapter 14).

✓ **Prepare updated wills.** When you marry, you should make or update your wills. Having a will is potentially more valuable when you're married, especially if you want to leave money to others in addition to your spouse, or if you have children for whom you need to name a guardian. Check out the nearby sidebar "Preparing wills and other important legal documents" for more guidance.

✓ **Review beneficiaries on investment and life insurance.** With retirement accounts and life insurance policies, you name beneficiaries to whom the money or value in those accounts will go in the event of your passing. When you marry, you should review and reconsider your beneficiaries.

After you're married, you and your spouse should set aside time once a year, or every few years, to discuss personal and financial goals for the years ahead. When you talk about where you want to go, you help ensure that you're both rowing your financial boat in unison.

Preparing wills and other important legal documents

When you have dependent children, a will is a must-have. The will names the guardian to whom you entrust your children if both you and your spouse die. Should both you and your spouse die without a will (a condition called *intestate*), the state (courts and social-service agencies) decides who will raise your children. Therefore, even if you can't decide at this time who you want to raise your children, you should at least appoint a trusted guardian who can decide for you.

Even if you have no dependents, having a will is wise because it provides your specific instructions on how to handle and distribute your possessions. If you die without a will, your state decides how to distribute your money and other property, according to state law. Therefore, your friends, distant relatives, and favorite charities would probably receive nothing. Without any living relatives, your money may go to the state government!

Without a will, your heirs are legally powerless, and the state may appoint an administrator to supervise the distribution of your assets at a fee of around 5 percent of your estate. A bond typically must also be posted at a cost of several hundred dollars.

A living will and a medical power of attorney are useful additions to a standard will. A *living will* tells your doctor what, if any, life-support measures you prefer. A medical (or healthcare) *power of attorney* grants authority to someone you trust to make decisions regarding your medical care options.

You don't need an attorney to make a legal will. Most attorneys, in fact, prepare wills and living trusts by using software packages! The simplest and least costly way to prepare a will, a living will, and a medical power of attorney is to use a high-quality, user-friendly software package such as those published by Nolo Press (www.nolo.com). What makes a will valid is that three people witness your signing it. Give copies of these documents to the guardians and executors you name.

Part III

Earning More (And Keeping More of What You Earn)

The 5th Wave   By Rich Tennant

"My plan is to build a diversified portfolio of stocks, money-market investments, and short-term bonds; contribute to a retirement account; and build capital toward a down payment on a house. Or, I'll buy a Corvette."

In this part . . .

1 help you make the most of your money. First, I discuss making the most of your career, continuing your education, and handling bouts of unemployment. Whether you're working or not, I help you with strategies for legally reducing your taxes. Finally, I cover the all-important territory of sound investing strategies and how to assemble and manage an investment portfolio.

Chapter 9

Making the Most of Your Career

In This Chapter

▶ Jump-starting your career

▶ Considering your options in the world of small business

▶ Being prepared for a career change

▶ Coping with unemployment

*W*hat's your most valuable asset? It's probably your future income-earning potential. That's why I devote this chapter to helping you make the most of your career and future employment. In addition to tips to jump-start your career, I discuss furthering your education and training, exploring your entrepreneurial options, and handling job changes and loss.

Getting Your Career Going

As you transition from school to the workforce, you can maximize your chances for financial and career success. This section discusses arranging your finances and making decisions to further invest in your education and training.

Putting everything in order

If you just graduated from school, or you're otherwise just entering the workforce, your increased income and reduction in educational expenses are probably a welcome relief — but they're no guarantee of future financial success. Here's how to start on the path to financial success when you first enter the job market:

✔ **Avoid consumer credit.** The use and abuse of consumer credit can cause long-term financial pain and hardship. Shun making purchases on credit cards that you can't pay for in full when the bill arrives. Here's the simple solution for running up outstanding credit card balances: Don't carry a credit card. If you need the convenience of making purchases with a piece of plastic, get a debit card (see Chapter 5).

✔ **Get in the habit of saving and investing.** I'm often asked, "At what age should a person start saving?" To me, that's similar to asking at what age you should start brushing your teeth. Well, when you have teeth to brush! So I say you should start saving and investing money from your first paycheck. Try saving 5 percent of every paycheck, and then eventually increase your saving to 10 percent. Ideally, you should put your savings into retirement accounts (through an automatic deduction) that offer tax benefits, unless you want to accumulate down-payment money for a home or small-business purchase. (You're probably not thinking about buying a new home or retiring, though, if you're just entering the job market.) If you're having trouble saving money, track your spending and make cutbacks as needed (refer to Chapters 3 and 4 for more assistance).

✔ **Get insured.** When you're young and healthy, imagining yourself feeling otherwise is hard. But because accidents and unexpected illnesses can strike at any age, forgoing health insurance coverage can be financially devastating. When you're in your first full-time job with limited benefits, buying disability coverage, which replaces income lost because of a long-term disability, is also wise. And as you begin to build your assets, make a will so that your assets go where you want them to in the event of your untimely passing. (Check out Part IV for more information about insurance.)

Educating and training your way to career success

The Bureau of Labor Statistics has data that clearly demonstrates that the more education a person has, the more money the person makes and the less likely the person is to be unemployed (see the most recent full year's data and chart in Figure 9-1).

Now, you must be careful applying group data to your own situation, because assuming that more education is *always* better would be inaccurate. But the data clearly shows that more education is *generally* better, as it enhances your employability and income-earning potential and reduces your chances of being unemployed.

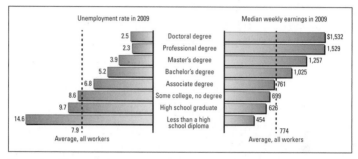

Figure 9-1: More education translates into lower unemployment rates and higher earnings.

Seeking value for your education dollars

You probably don't have an unlimited supply of money to spend on furthering your education and training. So, just as with buying anything else — computers, clothing, and so on — you should look for value when spending your education dollars. Value means getting the most (quality) for your money.

Keep the following pointers in mind to ensure you get value for your educational dollars:

  ✔ **Realize that you don't always get what you pay for.** Just because you spend more for education doesn't mean that you'll get better quality than something costing less.

  ✔ **Look beyond sticker prices.** Because of the availability of financial aid, including grants and scholarships you don't have to pay back, you can't simply compare the sticker price of various schools and assume that the price is your actual cost.

✔ **Be careful when examining rankings of colleges and which colleges' graduates earn the most.** Lots of data and rankings on the best colleges and universities are available. One challenge when evaluating such data is that many of the highest-rated schools are private and quite expensive, and they selectively admit the most qualified candidates. So their graduates tend to earn more. Be sure to compare what each school provides and what each costs after factoring in financial aid awards.

✔ **Consider employer assistance.** Check out what education assistance your employer may offer. Just be sure that it makes sense for you and your career to stay with that employer for whatever additional time may be required.

✔ **If you have specific fields of work in mind, research what education and training best prepares you.** Talk to folks currently in those fields and consider training programs as well as technical training programs where appropriate.

Investing in your career

In my work with financial counseling clients over the years and from observing friends and colleagues, I've witnessed plenty of people succeed in their careers. What did they have in common? They invested in their careers, and you can and should do the same. Some time-tested, proven ways to do that include

✔ **Networking:** Some people wait to network until they've been laid off or are really hungry to change jobs. Take an interest in what others do for a living and you'll benefit and grow from the experience, even if you choose to stay with your current employer or in your chosen field.

✔ **Making sure that you keep growing:** Whether it's reading high-quality books or other publications or taking some night courses, find ways to build on your knowledge base.

✔ **Considering the risk in the status quo:** Many folks are resistant to change and get anxious thinking about what could go wrong when taking a new risk. When I was ready to walk away from a six-figure consulting job with a prestigious firm and open my own financial counseling firm, a number of my relatives and friends thought I had lost my mind. I'm glad I didn't allow their fears and worries to dissuade me!

Exploring Entrepreneurial Options

Small business has generated more wealth than investing in the stock market or real estate. You can invest in small business by starting a business yourself, buying an existing business, or investing in someone else's small business. The following sections give you an overview in doing so.

Starting a small business

When you have self-discipline and a product or service you can sell, starting your own business can be both profitable and fulfilling. Before you start, consider the following:

- ✓ **Determine what skills and expertise you possess that you can use in your business.** You don't need a unique idea or invention to start a small business.

- ✓ **Begin exploring your idea by first developing a written business plan.** Such a plan should detail your product or service, how you're going to market it, your potential customers and competitors, and the economics of the business, including the start-up costs.

Of all the small-business investment options, starting your own business involves the most work. Although you can do this work on a part-time basis in the beginning, most people end up running their business full time — it's your new job, career, or whatever you want to call it.

In most people's eyes, starting a new business is the riskiest of all small-business investment options. But if you're going into a business that uses your skills and expertise, the risk isn't nearly as great as you may think. Many businesses can be started with little cash by leveraging your existing skills and expertise. You can build a valuable company and job if you have the time to devote to it. To begin your own business, check out the latest edition of *Small Business For Dummies* (Wiley), which I cowrote.

Purchasing a small business

If you don't have a specific product or service you want to sell but you're skilled at managing and improving the operations of a company, buying a small business may be for you. Finding and buying a good small business takes time and patience, so devote at least several months to the search. You may also need to enlist financial and legal advisors to help inspect the company, look over its financial statements, and hammer out a contract.

Good businesses don't come cheap. If the business is a success, the current owner has already removed the start-up risk from the business, so the price of the business should be at a premium to reflect this lack of risk. When you have the capital to buy an established business and you have the skills to run it, consider going this route.

Although you don't have to go through the riskier start-up period if you buy a small business, you'll likely need more capital to buy an established enterprise. You'll also need to be able to deal with stickier personnel and management issues. The organization's history and the way it works will predate your ownership of the business. If you don't like making hard decisions, firing people who don't fit with your plans, and getting people to change the way they do things, buying an existing business likely isn't for you.

Some people perceive buying an existing business as being safer than starting a new one. Buying someone else's business can actually be riskier. You're likely to shell out far more money upfront, in the form of a down payment. If you don't have the ability to run the business and it does poorly, you have more to lose financially. In addition, the business may be for sale for a reason — it may not be very profitable, it may be in decline, or it may generally be a pain in the neck to operate.

Investing in a small business

If you don't want the day-to-day headaches of being directly responsible for owning and managing a business but you do like the idea of profiting from a successful one, then investing in someone else's small business may be for you. Although this route may seem easier, few people are actually cut out to be investors in other people's businesses. The reason: Finding and analyzing opportunities isn't easy.

Are you astute at evaluating corporate financial statements and business strategies? Investing in a small, privately held company has much in common with investing in a publicly traded firm (as is the case when you buy stock), but it also has these differences:

- ✔ **Private firms aren't required to produce comprehensive, audited financial statements that adhere to certain accounting principles.** Thus, you have a greater risk of not having sufficient or accurate information when evaluating a small, private firm.

- ✔ **Unearthing private, small-business investing opportunities is harder.** The best private companies that are seeking investors generally don't advertise. Instead, they find prospective investors by networking with people such as business advisors. You can increase your chances of finding private companies to invest in by speaking with tax, legal, and financial advisors who work with small businesses. You can also find interesting opportunities through your own contacts or your experience within a given industry.

Consider investing in someone else's business only if you can afford to lose all of what you invest. Also, you should have sufficient assets so that whatever money you invest in small, privately held companies represents only a small portion (20 percent or less) of your total financial assets.

Changing Jobs or Careers

During your adult life, you'll almost surely change jobs — perhaps several times a decade. I hope that most of the time you change jobs by your own choice. But in today's increasingly global and rapidly changing economy, job security isn't great. Downsizing has affected even the most talented workers.

Always be prepared for a job change. No matter how happy you are in your current job, knowing that your world won't fall apart if you're not working tomorrow can give you an added sense of security and encourage openness to possibility. Whether you change your job by choice or necessity, the following financial maneuvers can help ease the transition:

✓ **Keep your spending lean.** Spending less than you earn always makes good financial sense, but if you're approaching a possible job change, spending less is even more important, particularly if you're entering a new field or starting your own company and you expect a short-term income dip. Many people view a lifestyle of thriftiness as restrictive, but ultimately, those thrifty habits can give you more freedom to do what you want to do.

✓ **Keep an emergency reserve fund.** You should have a "rainy day" fund to deal with emergencies and the inevitable curve balls that life throws your way. I suggest keeping it in a money market fund or savings account, and it should cover at least three months' worth of living expenses.

✓ **Evaluate the total financial picture when relocating.** At some point in your career, you may have the option of relocating. But don't call the moving company until you understand the financial consequences of such a move. You can't simply compare salaries and benefits between the two jobs. You also need to compare the cost of living between the two areas, which includes housing, commuting, state income and property taxes, food, utilities, and all the other major expenditure categories.

✓ **Track your job search expenses for tax purposes.** If you're seeking a new job in your current (or recently current) field of work, your job search expenses may be tax-deductible, even if you don't get a specific job you desire. If you're moving into a new career, your job search expenses aren't tax-deductible.

The Young and the Unemployed

Your job search may play out like a daytime drama, which is no surprise if you're having a difficult time finding a job. But being unemployed means that you need to be especially concerned with your personal finances. The following sections point out why unemployment strikes younger people harder and what you can do during this rough time.

Understanding how joblessness hits younger people harder

During the severe recession in the late 2000s, high unemployment rates were all over the news as the unemployment rate surpassed 10 percent in the United States. But that double-digit level of joblessness pales in comparison to the high level of unemployment for young people, especially those who are less well educated.

In late 2010, the national unemployment rate of around 9.5 percent hid the fact that some groups are hit much harder with unemployment than others. For example, people age 35 and older have an unemployment rate of less than 8 percent. Those ages 25 to 34 suffer a rate of nearly 11 percent, and those ages 16 to 24 have an unemployment rate in excess of 18 percent!

In terms of education, those without a high school diploma have an unemployment rate of about 14 percent, and high school graduates who have no college experience have an unemployment rate of around 11 percent. College graduates have by far the lowest unemployment — it's less than 4.5 percent.

Adding up all this data tells you that the typical out-of-work person tends to be young and not well educated. Although you can't do anything about your age, you can do something about your education (see the earlier section "Getting Your Career Going").

Accessing unemployment benefits

If you're laid off and unemployed, you should collect unemployment benefits if you're eligible. You must be actively seeking employment and meet any other eligibility requirements in your state.

The simplest way to find the state unemployment insurance office nearest you is to visit the Web site www.service locator.org and click "Unemployment Benefits" on the home page. CareerOneStop operates this site — a U.S. Department of Labor-sponsored Web site that provides "career resources and workforce information to job seekers, students, businesses, and workforce professionals to foster talent development in a global economy."

Unemployment benefits are provided at the state level, and each state has its own program. If you're turned down for benefits, be sure to clarify why, and don't be shy about appealing the decision if you feel there's a chance you may get approved if you're able to furnish more information.

Taking action

You can make the most of your finances and be best prepared to handle life's challenges if you stay on top of your financial affairs. That said, losing one's job often comes as a surprise and presents some unusual stresses. Here are some tips to keep in mind if you lose your job:

- ✔ **Batten down the hatches.** Evaluating and slashing your current level of spending may be necessary. Everything should be fair game, from how much you spend on housing to how often you eat out to where you do your grocery shopping. Avoid at all costs the temptation to maintain your level of spending by accumulating consumer debt.

- ✔ **Work at your job search a few hours daily but not on a full-time basis.** Searching for a job is hard work and creates stress for most people. You're probably not going to make the most of your job search by making it your full-time endeavor. Make some calls, arrange some appointments, send some résumés, and do some research on industries, companies, and organizations of interest every day. But I suggest doing so for no more than four to six hours per day. If you can find part-time or temporary work, spend some time doing that to earn some money and to break up the monotony of looking for work.

- ✔ **Try to exercise regularly.** Exercise clears the head and lifts your mood. Daily exercise is best, but if that's not possible, try to get some exercise at least every other day.

- ✔ **Eat healthfully.** As with exercise, eating a balanced and nutritious diet can go a long way toward maximizing your mental health and outlook.

Chapter 10

Taxes: Reduce Them or Else!

....

....

*T*axes are likely one of your largest expenses along with your housing costs. So you should be highly motivated to reduce your taxes within the boundaries of the law. And you need to understand enough of the tax laws and rules so that you don't get whacked with penalties and interest charges. This chapter can help you stay on the right side of the law and understand what strategies you can use to reduce your income taxes.

Understanding Taxable Income

Your *taxable income* is income on which you actually pay income taxes. Your employment income and the interest you earn on bank savings accounts and certificates of deposit (CDs) are all federally taxable. By contrast, interest paid on municipal bonds is generally not federally taxable. As I discuss later in this chapter, some income, such as from stock dividends and long-term capital gains, is taxed at lower rates than ordinary income.

Knowing your taxable income is important because it can help you focus on strategies for lowering it. When doing your federal income tax return, you calculate your taxable income by subtracting deductions from your income. Certain expenses, such as mortgage interest and property taxes, are deductible in the event that these itemized deductions exceed the standard deduction. (See the later section "Increasing Your Deductions" for more details.) When you contribute to qualified retirement plans, you also get a deduction, just as you do if you put money into a health savings account.

Comparing Marginal Taxes

My purpose in writing this chapter is to help you legally and permanently reduce your taxes. Understanding the tax system is the key to reducing your tax burden.

As an important starting point, you need to understand the concept of marginal tax rates. Get out your most recent year's federal and state income tax returns and look up the total taxes you paid that year. Many people don't know this amount (perhaps in part because it's too often a depressingly large number) but instead can tell me whether they got a refund. Remember — all a refund reflects is the repayment to you of some tax dollars because you overpaid your taxes during the year.

Regarding taxes, not all income is treated equally. This fact is far from self-evident. If you work for an employer and earn a constant salary during the course of a year, a steady and equal amount of federal and state taxes is deducted from each paycheck. Thus, it appears as though all that earned income is being taxed equally.

In reality, however, you pay less tax on your first dollars of earnings and more tax on your last dollars of earnings. Your *marginal tax rate* is the rate of tax you pay on your last, or highest, dollars of income. For example, if you're single and your taxable income totals $30,000 during 2010, you pay federal tax at the rate of 10 percent on the first $8,375 of taxable income and 15 percent on income between $8,375 and $34,000. Your marginal tax rate is 15 percent. Your total marginal rate includes your federal and state tax rates, as well as local income tax rates in the municipalities that have them. You can look up your state income tax rate in your current state income tax preparation booklet or on your state's government Web site. Table 10-1 shows the federal income tax brackets for single folks and married couples filing jointly for 2010.

Table 10-1 2010 Federal Income Tax Rates for Singles and Married Households Filing Jointly

Tax Rate	Single Filers	Married Filing Jointly
10%	less than $8,375	less than $16,750
15%	$8,375–$34,000	$16,750–$68,000
25%	$34,000–$82,400	$68,000–$137,300
28%	$82,400–$171,850	$137,300–$209,250
33%	$171,850–$373,650	$209,250–$373,650
35%	$373,650 or more	$373,650 or more

The marginal tax rate is a powerful concept that allows you to determine the additional taxes you have to pay on more income. Conversely, you can calculate the amount of taxes you save by reducing your taxable income, either by decreasing your income or by increasing your deductions.

Reducing Taxes on Work Income

When you earn money from work, you're supposed to pay income tax on that income. You can, of course, avoid taxes by illegal means, such as by not reporting such income, but you can very well end up paying a heap of penalties and extra interest charges on top of the taxes you owe. And you may even get tossed in jail. This section focuses on the legal ways to reduce your income taxes on work-related income.

Contributing to retirement plans

One way you can exclude money from your taxable income is by tucking it away in employer-based retirement plans, such as 401(k) or 403(b) accounts, or self-employed retirement plans, such as SEP-IRAs or Keoghs. Besides reducing your taxes, retirement plans help you build up a nest egg so that you don't have to work for the rest of your life.

If your combined federal and state marginal tax rate (see the earlier "Comparing Marginal Taxes" section) is, say, 25 percent and you contribute $1,000 to one of these plans, you reduce your federal and state taxes by $250. Contribute another $1,000, and your taxes drop another $250 (as long as you're still in the same marginal tax rate). And when your money is inside a retirement account, it can compound and grow without taxation. (Some employers offer an additional perk: free matching money simply for your contributing.)

Single taxpayers with an adjusted gross income (AGI) of less than $27,750 and married couples filing jointly with an AGI of less than $55,500 can earn a relatively new tax credit (claimed on Form 8880) for retirement account contributions. (*AGI* is your total wage, interest, dividend, and all other income minus retirement account contributions, self-employed health insurance, alimony paid, and losses from investments.) Unlike a deduction, a tax credit directly reduces your tax bill by the amount of the credit. This credit, which is detailed in Table 10-2, is a percentage of the first $2,000 you contribute to a retirement plan (or $4,000 on a joint return). The credit isn't available to those individuals under the age of 18, full-time students, or people who are claimed as dependents on someone else's tax return.

Table 10-2   Special Tax Credit for Retirement Plan Contributions

Singles Adjusted Gross Income	Married Filing Jointly Adjusted Gross Income	Tax Credit for Retirement Account Contributions
$0–$16,500	$0–$33,000	50%
$16,500–$18,000	$33,000–$36,000	20%
$18,000–$27,750	$36,000–$55,500	10%

Many people miss this great opportunity for reducing their taxes because they spend all (or too much of) their current employment income and, therefore, have nothing (or little) left to put into a retirement account. If you're in this predicament, you need to reduce your spending before you can contribute money to a retirement plan. (See Chapters 3 and 4 for advice on decreasing your spending.)

If your employer doesn't offer the option of saving money through a retirement plan, ask the benefits and human resource(s) person/department whether the company would consider offering such a plan. Alternatively, consider contributing to an individual retirement account (IRA), which may or may not be tax-deductible, depending on your circumstances. You should first maximize contributions to the previously mentioned tax-deductible accounts. (See Chapter 3 for more on all types of retirement accounts.)

Avoiding retirement account withdrawal penalties

Many young people object to funding retirement accounts because retirement seems so far away and because the money in retirement accounts, once contributed, is only accessible subject to penalties (10 percent federal plus whatever your state charges).

However, if you do put money into a retirement account, you can avoid these early withdrawal penalties under several different circumstances:

✔ You can make penalty-free withdrawals from individual retirement accounts for a first-time home purchase (limit of $10,000).

✔ Higher educational expenses for you, your spouse, your children, or your grandchildren.

✔ If you have major medical expenses (exceeding 7.5 percent of your income) or a disability, you may be exempt from the penalties under certain conditions.

✔ If you get into a financial pinch while you're still employed, be aware that some company retirement plans allow you to borrow against your balance.

This tactic is like loaning money to yourself — the interest payments go back into your account. (Important note: If you fail to repay the loan, it's classified as a withdrawal and subject to early withdrawal penalties.)

✔ If you lose your job and withdraw retirement account money simply because you need it to live on, the penalties do apply. However, if you're not working and you're earning so little income that you need to tap your retirement account, you surely fall into a low tax bracket. The lower income taxes you pay (when compared to the taxes you would have paid on that money had you not sheltered it in a retirement account in the first place) should make up for most or all of the penalty.

✔ The IRS allows you to withdraw money before age 59½ if you do so in equal, annual installments based on your life expectancy. The IRS has a table for looking up your life expectancy.

However, a retirement account may not be the wisest decision for you at this time. Good reasons not to fund a retirement account include:

- ✔ **You have a specific, shorter-term goal.** Such goals include saving to purchase a home or starting a business that necessitates having access to your money.

- ✔ **You're temporarily in a very low tax bracket.** This could happen, for example, if you lose your job for an extended period of time or are in school. (In these cases, you're unlikely to have lots of spare money to contribute to a retirement account anyway!) If you have some employment income, consider the Roth IRA (see Chapter 3).

Using health savings accounts

A more recent invention for reducing your taxable income and socking away money for future healthcare expenses is the *health savings account* (HSA). In fact, HSAs can offer superior tax savings versus retirement accounts because in addition to providing upfront tax breaks on contributions and tax-free accumulation of investment earnings, you can also withdraw money from HSAs tax-free so long as the money is used for healthcare costs. No other retirement accounts offer this triple tax-free benefit. For more details on HSAs, see Chapter 13.

Deducting self-employment expenses

When you're self-employed, you can deduct a multitude of expenses from your income before calculating the tax you owe. Sadly, many self-employed folks don't take all the deductions they're eligible for. In some cases, people simply aren't aware of the wonderful world of deductions. Others are worried that large deductions will increase the risk of an audit.

When you're self-employed, going it alone when dealing with your taxes is usually a mistake. You must educate yourself to make the tax laws work for you rather than against you. Spend some time finding out more about tax deductions; you'll be convinced that taking full advantage of your eligible deductions makes sense and saves you money. Hiring tax help is well worth your while, and recordkeeping is essential.

More items than you expect are deductible. If you buy a computer or office furniture, you can deduct those expenses. (Sometimes they need to be gradually deducted, or *depreciated,* over time.) Salaries for employees, the cost of office supplies, rent or mortgage interest for your office space, and phone/communications expenses are also generally deductible.

As a self-employed individual, you're responsible for the accurate and timely filing of all taxes owed on your income and employment taxes on your employees (if you have them) in order to avoid penalties. You need to make estimated tax payments on a quarterly basis. To pay taxes on your income, use Form 1040-ES. You can obtain this form, along with instructions, from the IRS (800-829-3676; www.irs.gov). The form comes with an estimated tax worksheet and four quarterly tax payment coupons. If you want to find the rules for withholding and submitting taxes from employees' paychecks, ask the IRS for Form 941, and for unemployment insurance, look for Form 940. And unless you're lucky enough to live in a state with no income taxes, you need to call your state's department of revenue or a similar entity for your state's estimated income tax package. Another alternative is to hire a payroll firm, such as ADP or Paychex, to do all this work for you.

When you pay with cash, following the paper trail for all the money you spent can be hard to do (for you and for the IRS, in the event you're ever audited). At the end of the year, how are you going to remember how much you spent for parking or client meals if you fail to keep a record? How will you survive an IRS audit without proper documentation?

Debit cards are accepted most places and provide a convenient paper trail. (Be careful about getting a debit card in your business's name, though, because some banks don't offer protection against fraudulent use of business debit cards.) Otherwise, you need a system or written record of your daily petty cash purchases. Most pocket calendars or daily organizers include ledgers that allow you to track these small purchases. If you aren't that organized, at least get receipts for cash transactions and stash them in a file folder in your desk. Or keep receipts in envelopes labeled with the month and year.

If your children, spouse, or other relatives help with some aspect of your business, consider paying them for the work. Besides showing them that you value their work, this practice may reduce your family's tax liability. For example, children are usually in a lower tax bracket. By shifting some of your income to your child, you cut your tax bill.

Increasing Your Deductions

Deductions are amounts you subtract from your adjusted gross income before calculating the tax you owe. The IRS gives you two methods for determining your total deductions and allows you to select the method that leads to greater deductions and lower taxes.

The two methods are as follows:

- ✔ **Standard deduction:** If you have a relatively simple financial life, taking the standard deduction is generally the better option. Those who are blind or who are age 65 or older get a slightly higher standard deduction.

- ✔ **Itemized deduction:** Itemizing your deductions on Schedule A of IRS Form 1040 is the other method for determining your allowable deductions. Itemizing tends to make more sense for those who earn a high income, own their own home (mortgage interest and property taxes are itemized deductions), and/or have unusually large expenses from medical bills, charitable contributions, or loss due to theft or catastrophe.

If you don't currently itemize, you may be surprised to discover that your state income taxes can be itemized. Also, when you pay a fee to the state to register and license your car, you can itemize a portion of the expenditure as a deduction (on Schedule A, "Personal Property Taxes"). The IRS allows you to deduct the part of the fee that relates to the value of your car. The state organization that collects the fee should be able to tell you what portion of the fee is deductible. (Some states detail on the invoice what portion of the fee is tax-deductible.)

Several states have state disability insurance funds. If you pay into these funds (check your W-2), you can deduct your payments as state and local income taxes on line 5 of Schedule A. You may also claim a deduction on this line for payments you make into your state's unemployment compensation fund.

A number of miscellaneous expenses are also deductible on Schedule A to the extent that they exceed 2 percent of your AGI (adjusted gross income). Most of these expenses relate to your job or career and the management of your finances:

✔ **Work-related educational expenses:** You may be able to deduct the cost of tuition, books, and travel to and from classes if your education is related to your career. Specifically, you can deduct these expenses if your course work improves your work skills. Courses required by law or your employer to maintain your position are deductible. Continuing education classes for professionals may also be deductible. *Note:* Educational expenses that lead to your moving into a new field or career are not deductible.

✔ **Expenses for job searches and career counseling:** After you obtain your first job, you may deduct legitimate costs related to finding another job within your field. You can even deduct the cost of courses and trips for new job interviews — even if you don't change jobs. And if you hire a career counselor to help you, you can deduct that cost as well.

✔ **Expenses related to your job that aren't reimbursed:** When you pay for your own subscriptions to trade journals to keep up with your field, or you buy a new desk and chair to ease back pain, you can deduct these costs. If your job requires you to wear special clothes or a uniform (for example, you're an EMT), you can deduct the cost of purchasing and cleaning these clothes, as long as they aren't suitable for wearing outside of work. When you buy a computer for use outside the office at your own expense, you may be able to deduct the cost if the computer is for the convenience of your employer, is a condition of your employment, and is used more than half the time for business. Union dues and membership fees for professional organizations are also deductible.

✔ **Investment and tax-related expenses:** Investment and tax-advisor fees are deductible, as are subscription costs for investment-related publications. Accounting fees for preparing your tax return or conducting tax planning during the year are deductible; legal fees related to your taxes are also deductible. If you purchase a home computer to track your investments or prepare your taxes, you can deduct that expense, too.

Lowering Investment Income Taxes

The distributions and profits on investments that you hold outside of tax-sheltered retirement accounts are exposed to taxation. Interest, dividends, and *capital gains* (profits from the sale of an investment at a price that's higher than the purchase price) are all taxed. The good news: You can take action to reduce the taxes in those accounts. This section explains some of the best methods for doing so.

Investing in tax-free money market funds and bonds

When you're in a high tax bracket, you may find that you come out ahead with tax-free investments. Tax-free investments pay investment income, which is exempt from federal tax, state tax, or both. Tax-free investments yield less than comparable investments that produce taxable income. But because of the difference in taxes, the earnings from tax-free investments can end up being greater than what you're left with from taxable investments.

Two tax-free options include the following. (See Chapter 11 for more details on tax-free investments.)

- ✔ **Money market funds:** Tax-free money market funds can be a better alternative to bank savings accounts, the interest on which is subject to taxation.

- ✔ **Bonds:** Likewise, tax-free bonds are intended to be longer-term investments that pay tax-free interest, so they may be a better more tax-efficient investment option for you than bank certificates of deposit, Treasury bills and bonds, and other investments that produce taxable income.

Selecting other tax-friendly investments

Too often, when selecting investments, people mistakenly focus on past rates of return, before-tax. The past, of course, is no guarantee of the future. Selecting an investment with a reportedly high rate of return without considering tax consequences is an even worse mistake because what you get to keep, after taxes, is what matters.

I call investments that appreciate in value and don't distribute much in the way of highly taxed income *tax-friendly.* (Some in the investment business use the term *tax-efficient.*) See Chapter 11 for more information on tax-friendly stocks and stock mutual funds.

Real estate is one of the few areas with privileged status in the tax code. In addition to deductions allowed for mortgage interest and property taxes, you can depreciate rental property to reduce your taxable income. *Depreciation* is a special tax deduction allowed for the gradual wear and tear on rental real estate. When you sell investment real estate, you may be eligible to conduct a tax-free exchange into a replacement rental property.

Making your profits long term

When you buy growth investments such as stocks and real estate, you should do so for the long term. The tax system rewards your patience with lower tax rates on your profits.

When you're able to hold on to a nonretirement account investment such as a stock, bond, or mutual fund for more than one year, you get a tax break if you sell that investment at a profit. Specifically, your profit is taxed under the lower capital gains tax rate schedule. If you're in the 25 percent or higher federal income tax bracket, you pay just 15 percent of your long-term capital gains' profit in federal taxes. (The same lower tax rate applies to qualified stock dividends.) If you're in the 10 or 15 percent federal income tax brackets, the long-term capital gains tax rate is 0 percent. (*Note:* As this book goes to press in late 2010, the tax laws may change for 2011, but those changes aren't yet clear. Visit my Web site, www. erictyson.com, for any updates.)

Enlisting Education Tax Breaks

The U.S. tax laws include numerous tax breaks for education-related expenditures. Here are the important tax-reduction opportunities you should know about for yourself and your kids if you have them:

✔ **Tax deductions for college expenses:** You may take up to a $2,500 tax deduction on IRS Form 1040 for college costs as long as your modified adjusted gross income (AGI) is less than $60,000 for single taxpayers and less than $120,000 for married couples filing jointly. (***Note:*** You may take a partial tax deduction if your AGI is between $60,000 and $75,000 for single taxpayers and between $120,000 and $150,000 for married couples filing jointly.)

✔ **Tax-free investment earnings in special accounts:** Money invested in *Education Savings Accounts* (ESAs) and in Section 529 plans is sheltered from taxation and is not taxed upon withdrawal as long as the money is used to pay for eligible education expenses. Subject to eligibility requirements, you may contribute up to $2,000 annually to ESAs. 529 plans allow you to sock away more than $200,000. Funding such accounts may harm your kid's potential financial aid.

✔ **Tax credits:** The American Opportunity and Lifetime Learning credits provide tax relief to low- and moderate-income earners facing education costs. The full credit (up to $2,500 per student) is available to individuals whose modified adjusted gross income is $80,000 or less, or $160,000 or less for married couples filing jointly. The credit is phased out for taxpayers above that. The credit can be claimed for expenses for the first four years of postsecondary education. You may be able to claim an American Opportunity tax credit in the same year in which you receive a distribution from either an ESA or 529, but you can't use expenses paid with a distribution from either an ESA or 529 as the basis for the American Opportunity credit.

Preparing Your Tax Return and Minimizing Your Taxes

Every year that you earn money, you'll probably complete a federal and state income tax return. Regardless of which approach you use to prepare and file your returns, you should take financial moves during the year to reduce your taxes.

Here are some resources to help:

✔ **IRS materials and guidance:** If you have a relatively simple, straightforward situation, filing your tax return on your own by using IRS instructions and pamphlets is okay. However, recognize that their publications don't go out of their way to highlight tax-reduction opportunities. And if you call the IRS with questions, know that the IRS has been known to give wrong information from time to time. For you Web surfers, the Internal Revenue Service Web site (www.irs.gov) is among the better Internet tax sites, believe it or not.

✔ **Preparation and advice guides:** Books about tax preparation and tax planning that highlight common problem areas and are written in clear, simple English are invaluable. They supplement the official instructions, not only by helping you complete your return correctly but also by showing you how to save as much money as possible. Please visit my Web site (www.erictyson.com) for up-to-date recommendations.

✔ **Software:** If you have access to a computer, good tax-preparation software can be helpful. TurboTax is a good program that I've reviewed. If you go the software route, I highly recommend having a good tax advice book by your side.

✔ **Professional hired help:** Competent tax preparers and advisors can save you money by identifying tax-reduction strategies you may overlook. They can also help reduce the likelihood of an audit, which can be triggered by blunders. Tax practitioners come with varying backgrounds, training, and credentials. The more training and specialization a tax practitioner has (and the more affluent his clients), the higher his hourly fee usually is. Fees and competence vary greatly.

Enrolled agents (EAs) must pass IRS scrutiny in order to be called an *enrolled agent*. This license allows the agent to represent you before the IRS in the event of an audit. Continuing education is also required; the training is generally longer and more sophisticated than it is for a typical preparer. Returns that require some of the more common schedules (such as Schedule A for deductions) cost about $200+ to prepare. To obtain names and telephone numbers of EAs in your area, contact the National Association of Enrolled Agents (NAEA) at 202-822-6232 or www.naea.org.

If you're self-employed and/or you file lots of other schedules, you may want to consider hiring a certified public accountant (CPA). But you don't need to do so year after year. If your situation grows complex one year and then stabilizes, consider getting help for the perplexing year and then using preparation guides, software, or a lower-cost preparer or enrolled agent in the future. CPAs go through significant training and examination before receiving the CPA credential. In order to maintain this designation, a CPA must also complete a fair number of continuing education classes every year. CPA fees vary tremendously. Most charge $100+ per hour, but CPAs at large companies and in high-cost-of-living areas tend to charge somewhat more.

Chapter 11

Successful Investing Principles

*O*ne of the most important financial tasks you'll tackle in your 20s and later adult years is investing money you've worked hard to earn and save. Investing wisely takes knowledge, discipline, and a sound philosophy. The good news: This chapter can help you get on the right path.

Understanding Investments

Ignore, for a moment, all the specific investments you've ever heard of. Having a basic grasp of the investment world is important, so I simplify it for you in the following sections. You have two major investment choices: You can be a lender or an owner.

Examining bonds and other lending investments

When you invest your money in a bank certificate of deposit (CD), a Treasury bill, or a bond issued by a company — such as the global chemical giant DuPont, for example — you're a *lender.* In each case, you lend your money to an organization — a bank, the federal government, or DuPont. The organization pays you an agreed-upon rate of interest for lending your money and promises to return your original investment (the principal) on a specific date.

Getting paid all the interest in addition to getting back your original investment (as promised) is your hoped-for outcome when you make a lending investment. Given that the investment landscape is littered with carcasses of failed investments, however, this result isn't guaranteed. The following sections outline what happens when you invest in bonds and discuss some lending drawbacks.

Investing in bonds

When you invest in a newly issued bond, you lend your money to an organization. The bond includes a specified *maturity date* — the time at which the principal is repaid — and a particular *interest rate,* or what's known as a *coupon.* This rate is fixed on most bonds. So, for example, if you buy a ten-year, 5 percent bond issued by Boeing, the aircraft manufacturer, you're lending your money to Boeing for ten years at an interest rate of 5 percent per year. (Bond interest is usually paid in two equal, semiannual installments.)

Some types of bonds have higher yields than others, but the risk-reward relationship remains intact. A bond generally pays you a higher rate of interest when it has a

- ✔ **Lower credit rating:** To compensate for the higher risk of default and the higher likelihood of losing your investment

- ✔ **Longer-term maturity:** To compensate for the risk that you'll be unhappy with the bond's set interest rate if the market level of interest rates moves up

A bond's value generally moves opposite of the directional change in interest rates. For example, if you're holding a bond issued at 5 percent and rates increase to 6 percent on comparable, newly issued bonds, your bond decreases in value. (Why would anyone want to buy your bond at the price you paid if it yields just 5 percent when 6 percent can be obtained elsewhere?)

Bonds differ from one another in the following major ways:

✔ **The type of institution to which you lend your money:**
With *municipal bonds,* you lend your money to a state or
local government or agency; with *Treasuries,* you lend
your money to the federal government; with *corporate
bonds,* you lend your money to a corporation.

✔ **The credit quality of the borrower to which you lend
your money:** *Credit quality* is a measurement of the
likelihood that the borrower will default on the interest
and principal you're owed. Knowing this information is
important because higher credit rating bonds are generally safer but pay lower rates of interest.

✔ **The length of the bond's maturity:** *Short-term* bonds
mature within 5 years, *intermediate* bonds mature within
5 to 10 years, and *long-term* bonds mature within 30
years. Longer-term bonds generally pay higher yields but
fluctuate more with changes in interest rates.

✔ **The bond's callability:** *Callability* means that the bond's
issuer can decide to pay you back earlier than the previously agreed-upon date. This event usually occurs when
interest rates fall and the bond issuer wants to issue
new, lower-interest-rate bonds to replace the higher-rate
bonds outstanding. To compensate you for early repayment, the bond's issuer typically gives you a small premium over what the bond is currently valued at.

Considering the downsides to lending

Many folks think that lending investments are safe and without risk, which is wrong. Lending money has the following
disadvantages:

✔ **You may not get what you're promised.** When a company goes bankrupt, for example, you can lose all or part
of your original investment.

✔ **Your money's purchasing power may be reduced by the
ravages of inflation.** Many folks have grown complacent
with the low inflation the United States has enjoyed for
quite some time. But what if inflation increases to 6 percent per year, or even 10 percent per year, as it last did
in the early 1980s? After a decade of that much inflation,
the purchasing power of your money drops 44 percent at
6 percent annual inflation and a whopping 61 percent at
10 percent yearly inflation. Also, the value of a bond may
drop below what you paid for it if interest rates rise or the
quality/risk of the issuing company declines.

> ✔ **You don't share in the upside of the organization to which you lend your money.** If a company grows in size and profits, your principal and interest rate don't grow along with it; they stay the same. Of course, such success should ensure that you get your promised interest and principal.

Exploring stocks, real estate, and small-business investments

The three best ways to build long-term wealth are to invest in ownership investments: stocks, real estate, and small business. I've found this to be true from observing many clients and other investors and from my own personal experiences. The following sections outline these three ways in greater depth.

Socking your money away in stocks

Stocks, which represent shares of ownership in a company, are the most common ownership investment vehicle. You're an *owner* when you invest your money in an asset, such as a company or real estate, that has the ability to generate earnings or profits. Suppose that you own 100 shares of Verizon Communications, Inc., stock. With billions of shares of stock outstanding, Verizon is a mighty big company — your 100 shares represent a tiny piece of it.

What do you get for your small slice of Verizon? Although you don't get free calling, you do as a stockholder share in the company's profits in the form of dividends (quarterly payments to shareholders from the company) and an increase (you hope) in the stock price if the company grows and becomes more profitable. Of course, you receive these benefits if things are going well. If Verizon's business declines, your stock may be worth less (or even worthless!).

As the economy grows and companies grow with it and earn greater profits, stock prices and dividend payouts on those stocks generally increase. Stock prices and dividends don't move in lockstep with earnings, but over the years, the relationship is pretty close.

In fact, the *price-earnings ratio* — which measures the level of stock prices relative to (or divided by) company earnings — of U.S. stocks has averaged approximately 15 the past two centuries (although it tends to be higher during periods of low inflation). A price-earnings ratio of 15 simply means that shares of a company's stock, on average, are selling at about 15 times the company's earnings per share.

When companies go public, they issue shares of stock that people can purchase on the major stock exchanges, such as the New York Stock Exchange. Companies that issue stock are called *publicly held companies.* By contrast, some companies are *privately held,* which means that they've elected to sell their stock only to senior management and a small number of invited, affluent investors. Privately held companies' stocks don't trade on a stock exchange, thus limiting who can be a shareholder.

Not only can you invest in company stocks that trade on the U.S. stock exchanges, but you can also invest in stocks overseas. Many investing opportunities exist overseas. If you look at the total value of all stocks outstanding worldwide, the value of U.S. stocks is in the minority.

 A good reason for investing in international stocks is that when you confine your investing to U.S. securities, you miss a world of opportunities, like taking advantage of business growth in other countries, as well as diversifying your portfolio even further. (For more on diversification, see the later section "Spreading Your Investment Risks.") International securities markets traditionally haven't moved in tandem with U.S. markets.

 Investing in the stock market involves setbacks and difficult periods, but the overall journey should be worth the effort. Over the past two centuries, the U.S. stock market has produced an annual average rate of return of about 10 percent. However, as anyone who invested in stocks experienced firsthand in the late 2000s, stocks can drop sharply — worldwide, stocks were sliced approximately in half during the down market that ended in early 2009. So if you can withstand down markets here and there over the course of many years, the stock market is a proven place to invest for long-term growth.

You can invest in stocks (and bonds, which I discuss earlier in this chapter) by making your own selection of individual stocks or by letting a mutual (or exchange-traded) fund do the selecting for you.

Investing in individual stocks

Who wouldn't want to own shares in the next hot stock? Few things are more financially satisfying than investing in a stock like Apple that multiplies your money many times over the years.

But investing in individual stocks entails numerous pitfalls:

✔ **You may fool yourself (or let others fool you) into thinking that picking and following individual companies and their stocks is simple and requires little time.**

When you're considering the purchase of an individual security, you should spend a significant amount of time doing research. You need to know a lot about the company in which you're thinking about investing. Relevant questions to ask about the company include: What products does it sell? What are its prospects for future growth and profitability? How much debt does it have? You need to do your homework not only before you make your initial investment but also on an ongoing basis for as long as you hold the investment. Research takes your valuable free time and sometimes costs money.

✔ **Your emotions will probably get in your way.** Analyzing financial statements, corporate strategy, and competitive position requires great intellect and insight. However, those skills aren't nearly enough. Will you have the stomach to hold on after what you thought was a sure-win stock plunges 50 percent? Will you have the courage to dump such a stock if your new research suggests that the plummet is the beginning of the end rather than just a bump in the road? When your money's on the line, emotions often undermine your ability to make sound, long-term decisions. Few people have the psychological constitution to handle the financial markets.

✔ **You're less likely to diversify.** Unless you have tens of thousands of dollars to invest in dozens of different stocks, you probably can't cost-effectively afford to develop a diversified portfolio. When investing in stocks, for example, you should hold companies in different industries and different companies within an industry. By not diversifying, you unnecessarily add to your risk. (For more on diversification, see the later section "Spreading Your Investment Risks.")

> ✓ **You'll face accounting and bookkeeping hassles.** When you invest in individual securities outside retirement accounts, every time you sell a security, you must report that transaction on your tax return.

Investing in individual securities should be done only by those who really enjoy doing it and are aware of and willing to accept the risks in doing so. Researching individual stocks can be more than a full-time job, and if you choose to take this path, remember that you'll be competing against the professionals who do so on a full-time basis. I recommend that you limit your individual stock picking to no more than 20 percent of your overall investments.

Discovering the advantages of mutual funds and ETFs

Mutual funds (investment pools that hold a collection of securities such as bonds and stocks) span the spectrum of risk and potential returns, from stable value money market funds (which are similar to savings accounts) to bond funds (which generally pay higher yields than money market funds but fluctuate with changes in interest rates) to stock funds (which offer the greatest potential for appreciation but also the greatest short-term volatility).

Exchange-traded funds (ETFs) are similar to mutual funds except that they trade on a major stock exchange and, unlike mutual funds, can be bought and sold during the trading day. The best ETFs have low fees, and like an index fund (which invests in a fixed mix of securities that track a specific market index), they invest to track the performance of a stock market index.

Efficiently managed mutual funds and exchange-traded funds, if properly selected, are a low-cost way for investors of both modest and substantial means to hire professional money managers. Over the long haul, you're not going to beat full-time professional managers who invest in securities of the same type and risk level.

Generating wealth with real estate

Real estate is another financially rewarding and time-honored ownership investment. Real estate can produce profits when you rent it for more than the expense of owning the property, or you sell it at a price higher than what you paid for it. I know numerous successful real estate investors (myself included) who've earned excellent long-term profits.

Over the generations, real estate owners and investors have enjoyed rates of return comparable to those produced by the stock market. However, like stocks, real estate goes through good and bad performance periods. Most people who make money investing in real estate do so because they invest over many years and do their homework when they buy to ensure that they purchase good property at an attractive price.

The value of real estate depends not only on the particulars of the individual property but also on the health and performance of the local economy. When companies in the community are growing and more jobs are being produced at higher wages, real estate does well. When local employers are laying people off and excess housing is vacant because of overbuilding, rent and property values fall, as they did in the late 2000s.

 Buying your own home is a good place to start investing in real estate. The *equity* in your home (the difference between the home's market value and the loan you owe on it) that builds over the years can become a significant part of your net worth. Over your adult life, owning a home should be less expensive than renting a comparable home. See Chapter 7 for the details on buying and financing your home.

Real estate's attributes

Real estate differs from most other investments in several respects. Here are real estate's unique attributes:

- ✔ **Usability:** Real estate is the only investment you can use (living in or renting out) to produce income. You can't live in a stock, bond, or mutual fund!

- ✔ **Less buildable land:** The demand for land and housing continues to grow with population growth. Scarcer land propels real estate prices higher over the long term.

- ✔ **Zoning determinations:** Local government regulates the zoning of property, and zoning determines what a property can be used for. In most communities, local zoning boards are against big growth. This position bodes well for future real estate values. Also know that in some cases, a particular property may not have been developed to its full potential. If you can figure out how to develop the property, you can reap large profits.

- ✔ **Leverage with debt usage:** Real estate is also different from other investments because you can borrow a lot of money to buy it — up to 80 percent or more of the property's value. This borrowing is known as exercising *leverage:* With an investment of 20 percent down, you're able to purchase and own a much larger investment. If the value of your real estate goes up, you make money on your investment and on all the money you borrowed.

✔ **Diamonds in the rough:** Real estate markets can be inefficient at times. Information isn't always easy to come by, and you may encounter a highly motivated or uninformed seller. Do your homework and you may be able to purchase a property below its fair market value.

✔ **Favorable tax treatment:** The tax code preferentially provides additional tax deductions, exclusions, or deferrals of taxes on gains on many types of real estate that aren't available on other types of investments.

Just as with any other investment, real estate has its drawbacks. Buying and selling a property takes time and is costly. When you're renting property, you discover firsthand the occasional headaches of being a landlord. And especially in the early years of rental property ownership, the property's expenses may exceed the rental income, producing a net cash drain.

Attractive real estate investments

You can invest in homes or small apartment buildings and then rent them out. In the long run, investment-property buyers usually see their rental income increase faster than their expenses and the value of their property increase.

When selecting real estate for investment purposes, remember that local economic growth is the fuel for housing demand. In addition to a vibrant and diverse job base, you want to look for limited supplies of both existing housing and land on which to build. When you identify potential properties in which you may want to invest, run the numbers to understand the cash demands of owning the property and the likely profitability.

If you don't want to be a landlord — one of the biggest drawbacks of investment real estate — consider *real estate investment trusts* (REITs). REITs are diversified real estate investment companies that purchase and manage rental real estate for investors. A typical REIT invests in different types of property, such as shopping centers, apartments, and other rental buildings. You can invest in REITs either by purchasing them directly on the major stock exchanges or by investing in a real estate mutual fund that invests in numerous REITs. For more information, check out my book, *Real Estate Investing For Dummies* (Wiley).

Going the small-business investment route

Many folks have also built substantial wealth through small business. You can participate in small business in a variety of ways. You can start your own business, buy and operate an existing business, or simply invest in promising small businesses. See Chapter 9 for more details.

Getting a Handle on Investment Risks

Many investors have a simplistic understanding of what risk means and how to apply it to their investment decisions. Having a firm handle on investment risk and what it means to you in your 20s and as you age is important.

For example, when compared to the gyrations of the stock market, a bank savings account may seem like a less risky place to put your money. Over the long term, however, the stock market usually beats the rate of inflation, while the interest rate on a savings account does not. Thus, if you're saving your money for a long-term goal like retirement, a savings account can be a "riskier" place to put your money than a diversified stock portfolio. The following sections take a closer look at determining what you want and identifying potential risks.

Establishing goals and risks

Before you select a specific investment, first determine your investment needs and goals. Ask yourself: Why are you saving money? What are you going to use it for? Establishing objectives is important because the expected use of the money helps you determine which investments to choose.

For example, suppose you've been accumulating money for a down payment on a home you want to buy in a few years.

You can't afford much risk with that money. You're going to need that money sooner rather than later. Putting that money in the stock market, then, is foolish because the stock market can drop a lot in a year or over several consecutive years.

By contrast, when saving toward a longer-term goal that's decades away, such as retirement, you're better able to make riskier investments, because your holdings have more time to bounce back from temporary losses or setbacks. You may want to consider investing in growth investments, such as stocks, in a retirement account that you leave alone for many years.

Comparing the risks of stocks and bonds

Given the relatively higher historic returns for ownership investments like stocks, some people think that they should put all their money in stocks and real estate. So what's the catch?

The risk with ownership investments is the short-term drops in their value. During the last century, stocks declined, on average, by more than 10 percent once every five years. Drops in stock prices of more than 20 percent occurred, on average, once every ten years. Real estate prices suffer similar periodic setbacks.

Therefore, in order to earn those generous long-term returns from ownership investments like stocks and real estate, you must be willing to tolerate volatility. You absolutely *should not* put all your money in the stock or real estate market. You shouldn't invest your emergency money or money you expect to use within the next five years in such volatile investments.

The shorter the time period that you have for holding your money in an investment, the less likely growth-oriented investments like stocks are to beat out lending-type investments like bonds.

When you invest in stocks and other growth-oriented investments, you must accept the volatility of these investments. That said, you can take several actions, which I discuss in this chapter and in Chapter 12, to greatly reduce your risk when investing in these higher potential–return investments. Invest the money that you have earmarked for the longer term in these vehicles. Minimize the risk of these investments through diversification. Don't buy just one or two stocks; buy a number of stocks. Keep reading for more information about diversification.

Spreading Your Investment Risks

Diversification is a powerful investment concept. It refers to placing your money in different investments with returns that aren't completely correlated. This is a fancy way of saying that when some of your investments are down in value, odds are that others are up in value.

To decrease the chances of all your investments getting clobbered at the same time, put your money in different types of investments, such as bonds, stocks, real estate, and small business. You can further diversify your investments by investing in domestic as well as international markets.

The following sections point out why diversifying your investments is important, how you can do it, and why you should avoid the temptation to toss them during down times.

Understanding why diversification is key

Within a given class of investments, such as stocks, investing in different types of that class (such as different types of stocks) that perform well under various economic conditions is important. For this reason, mutual funds, which are diversified portfolios of securities such as stocks or bonds, are a highly useful investment vehicle. When you buy into a mutual fund, your money is pooled with the money of many others and invested in a vast array of stocks or bonds.

Diversification reduces the volatility in the value of your whole portfolio. In other words, your portfolio can achieve the same rate of return that a single investment might typically provide with less fluctuation in value.

Keep in mind that no one, no matter whom he works for or what credentials he has, can guarantee returns on an investment. You can do good research and get lucky, but no one is free from the risk of losing money. Diversification allows you to reduce the risk of unnecessarily large losses from your investments.

Allocating your assets

Asset allocation refers to how you spread your investing dollars among different investment options (stocks, bonds, money market accounts, and so on). Over the long term, the asset allocation decision is the most important determinant of total return and risk for a diversified portfolio. Before you can intelligently decide how to allocate your assets, you need to ponder a number of issues, including your present financial situation, your goals and priorities, and the pros and cons of various investment options.

Although stocks and real estate offer attractive long-term returns, they can sometimes suffer significant declines. Thus, these investments aren't suitable for money that you think you may want or need to use within, say, the next five years.

 Money market funds and shorter-term bond investments are good places to keep money that you expect to use soon. Everyone should have a reserve of money — about three to six months' worth of living expenses in a money market fund — that they can access in an emergency. Shorter-term bonds or bond mutual funds can serve as a higher-yielding, secondary emergency cushion.

Investing money for retirement is a classic long-term goal that most people have. Your current age and the number of years until you retire are the biggest factors to consider when allocating money for long-term purposes. The younger you are and the more years you have before retirement, the more comfortable you should be with growth-oriented (and more volatile) investments, such as stocks and investment real estate. Bonds can also be useful for diversification purposes. For example, when investing for retirement, placing a portion of your money in bonds helps buffer stock market declines.

 A useful guideline fvor dividing or allocating your money between longer-term-oriented growth investments, such as stocks, and more-conservative lending investments, such as bonds, is to subtract your age from 110 (or 120 if you want to be aggressive; 100 to be more conservative) and invest the resulting percentage in stocks. You then invest the remaining amount in bonds.

For example, if you're 25, you invest from 75 (100 – 25) to 95 (120 – 25) percent in stocks. You invest the portion left over — 5 to 25 percent — in bonds. Consider allocating a percentage of your stock fund money to overseas investments: at least 20 percent to as much as 50 percent for more aggressive investors.

Holding onto your investments and shunning the herd

The allocation of your investment dollars should be driven by your goals and desire to take risk. As you get older, gradually scaling back on the riskiness (and, therefore, growth potential) of your portfolio generally makes sense.

Don't tinker with your portfolio daily, weekly, monthly, or even annually. Every three to five years or so, you may want to rebalance your holdings to get your mix to a desired asset allocation, as I discuss in the preceding section. Don't trade with the hopes of buying into a hot investment and selling your losers. Jumping onto a "winner" and dumping a "loser" may provide some short-term psychological comfort, but in the long term, such an investment strategy often produces subpar returns.

When an investment gets front-page coverage and everyone is talking about its stunning rise, it's definitely time to take a reality check. The higher the value of an investment rises, the greater the danger that it's overpriced. Its next move may be downward.

During the late 1990s, for example, many technology and Internet stocks had spectacular rises, thus attracting a lot of attention. However, the fact that the U.S. economy is increasingly becoming technology-based doesn't mean that any price you pay for a technology stock is fine. Some investors who neglected to do basic research and bought into the attention-grabbing, high-flying technology stocks lost 80 percent or more of their investments in the early 2000s — ouch!

Conversely, when things look bleak (as when stocks in general suffered significant losses in the early 2000s and then again in the late 2000s), giving up hope is easy — who wants to lose money? However, investors who forget about their overall asset allocation plan and panic and sell after a major decline miss out on a potential rebound in the market and a tremendous buying opportunity. We like buying televisions, computers, and cars on sale. Yet when the stock market is having a sale, many investors panic and sell instead of looking for bargains. Have courage and don't follow the herd.

Don't let a poor string of events sour you on stock investing. History has repeatedly proven that continuing to buy stocks during down markets increased long-term returns. Throwing in the towel is the worst thing you can do in a slumping market. And don't waste time trying to find a way to beat the system. Buy and hold a diversified portfolio of stocks. The financial markets reward investors for accepting risk and uncertainty.

Selecting an Investment Firm

Thousands of firms sell investments and manage money. Banks, mutual fund companies, securities brokerage firms, insurance companies, and others all want your money. I recommend that you do business with investment companies that

- ✔ **Offer the best value investments in comparison to their competitors.** Value is the combination of performance (including service) and cost. Commissions, management fees, maintenance fees, and other charges can turn a high-performance investment into a mediocre or poor one.

- ✔ **Employ representatives who don't have an inherent self-interest in steering you into a particular type of investment.** Give preference to investing firms that don't tempt their employees to push one investment over another in order to generate more fees. If the investment firm's people are paid on commission, be careful.

Mutual funds are an ideal investment vehicle for most investors. *No-load* mutual fund companies are firms through which you can invest in mutual funds without paying sales commissions, so all your invested dollars go to work in the mutual funds you choose.

Discount brokers generally pay the salaries of their brokers. *Discount brokers* are simply brokers without major conflicts of interest. Of course, like any other for-profit enterprise, they're in business to make money, but they're much less likely to steer you wrong for their own benefit.

In Chapter 12, I name names and recommend some of the best investments to utilize.

Evaluating Pundits and Experts

Believing that you can increase your investment returns by following the prognostications of certain gurus is a common mistake that some investors make, especially during more trying and uncertain times. Many people want to believe that some experts can predict the future of the investment world and keep them out of harm's way.

During the financial crisis of the late 2000s, all sorts of pundits were coming out of the woodwork, claiming that they had predicted what was unfolding. And when bad things were happening, commentators were all over the place predicting what would happen next.

The sad part about hyped articles with hyped predictions is that they cause some individual investors to panic and do the wrong thing, like selling good assets such as stocks at depressed prices. The media shouldn't irresponsibly publicize hyped predictions, especially without clearly and accurately disclosing the predictor's track record. Don't fall victim to such hype.

Ignore the predictions and speculations of self-proclaimed gurus and investment soothsayers. Commentators and experts who publish predictive commentaries and newsletters and who are interviewed in the media can't predict the future. The few people who have a slight leg up on everyone else aren't going to share their investment secrets — they're too busy investing their own money! If you have to believe in something to offset your fears, believe in good information and proven investment managers.

My Web site, www.erictyson.com, provides excerpts and updates from the best newsletters to which I subscribe and read. Also check out the "Guru Watch" section of my site in which I evaluate commonly quoted gurus and expose their real records.

Chapter 12

Portfolios for a Purpose

● ●

In This Chapter

▶ Choosing how to invest nonretirement account money

▶ Investing inside retirement accounts

▶ Paying for education costs

● ●

*I*n Chapter 11, I discuss the principles of intelligent invest-ing. This chapter takes you a step further to help you match your investments to specific goals.

Before You Begin Investing

Before you cast your investment line, consider the following two often-overlooked ways to put your money to work and earn higher returns without much risk:

✔ **Pay off high-interest debt.** If, for example, you have credit card debt outstanding at 14 percent interest, paying off that loan is the same as putting your money to work in an investment with a sure 14 percent annual return. Remember that the interest on consumer debt isn't tax-deductible, so you actually need to earn more than 14 percent investing your money elsewhere in order to net 14 percent after paying taxes.

✔ **Fund retirement accounts.** If you work for a company that offers a retirement savings plan such as a 401(k), fund it at the highest level you can manage. If you earn self-employment income, consider SEP-IRAs and Keogh plans. (I discuss the tax benefits of funding retirement plans options in Chapter 10.) Keep money for shorter-term goals, like buying a car or a home, in separate, much more liquid, accounts.

Investing Nonretirement Account Money

When you invest money outside a retirement account, those investments are exposed to taxation. Therefore, you must understand the tax features of your situation and your investment choices.

To decide between comparable taxable and tax-free investments, you need to know your *marginal tax bracket* (the tax rate you pay on an extra dollar of taxable income) and each investment's interest rate or yield. (See Chapter 10 to understand your tax bracket.)

In the sections that follow, I give specific advice about investing your money while keeping an eye on taxes.

Emergency money

When you have a few thousand dollars or less, your simplest path is to keep this money in a local bank or credit union. Look first to the institution where you keep your checking account. Keeping this stash of money in your checking account, rather than in a separate savings account, makes financial sense if the extra money helps you avoid monthly service charges when your balance occasionally dips below the minimum. Compare the service charges on your checking account with the interest earnings from a savings account.

Another option to consider is putting your money into a *money market fund,* a type of mutual fund, the best of which are usually superior to bank savings accounts because they pay higher yields than bank savings accounts and allow check-writing. And if you're in a high tax bracket, you can select a tax-free money market fund, which pays interest that's free from federal and/or state tax — something you can't get with a bank savings account.

The yield on a money market fund is an important consideration. The operating expenses deducted before payment of dividends is the single biggest determinant of yield. All other things being equal, lower operating expenses translate into higher yields for you. With interest rates as low as they are these days, seeking out money funds with the lowest operating expenses is essential.

Doing most or all of your fund shopping (money market and otherwise) at one good fund company can reduce the clutter in your investing life. Chasing after a slightly higher yield offered by another company is sometimes not worth the extra paperwork and administrative hassle. On the other hand, there's no reason why you can't invest in funds at multiple firms (as long as you don't mind the extra paperwork), using each for its relative strengths.

Most mutual fund companies don't have many local branch offices, so you may have to open and maintain your money market mutual fund through the fund's toll-free phone line, Web site, or the mail. Distance has its advantages. Because you can conduct business by mail, the Internet, and the phone, you don't need to go schlepping into a local branch office to make deposits and withdrawals. I'm happy to report that I haven't visited a bank office in many years.

Despite the distance between you and your mutual fund company, your money is still accessible via check-writing, and you can also have money wired to your local bank on any business day. Don't fret about a deposit being lost in the mail; it rarely happens, and no one can legally cash a check made payable to you, anyway. Just be sure to endorse the check with the notation "for deposit only" under your signature.

Long-term money

If you plan to invest outside retirement accounts, asset allocation for these accounts should depend on how comfortable you are with risk and how much time you have until you plan to use the money. That's not because you won't be able to sell these investments on short notice if necessary. Investing money in a more volatile investment is simply riskier if you need to liquidate it in the short term.

For example, suppose that you're saving money for a down payment on a house in about one to two years. If you had put this money into the U.S. stock market near the beginning of one of the stock market's major downturns (such as what happened in the early 2000s and then again in the late 2000s), you'd have been mighty unhappy. You would have seen a substantial portion of your money and home-buying dreams vanish.

In the sections that follow, I walk you through common investments for longer-term purposes.

Defining your time horizons

I organize the different investment options in the remainder of this section by time frame and by your tax situation. Following are summaries of the different time frames associated with each type of fund:

- ✔ **Short-term investments:** These investments are suitable for saving money for a home or some other major purchase within a few years. When investing for the short term, look for liquidity and stability — features that rule out real estate and stocks. Recommended investments include shorter-term bond funds, which are higher-yielding alternatives to money market funds. If interest rates increase, these funds will likely drop in value, but relatively less than longer-term bond funds. I also discuss Treasury bonds and certificates of deposit (CDs) later in this section.

- ✔ **Intermediate-term investments:** These investments are appropriate for more than a few years but less than ten years. Investments that fit the bill are intermediate-term bonds and well-diversified balanced funds (which include some stocks as well as bonds).

- ✔ **Long-term investments:** If you have a decade or more for investing your money, you can consider a portfolio that's balanced between bonds and potentially higher-return (and therefore riskier) investments. Stocks, real estate, and other growth-oriented investments can earn the most money if you're comfortable with the risk involved.

Buying Treasuries direct

Like a few other countries, the U.S. Treasury offers inflation-indexed government bonds. Because a portion of these Treasury bonds' return is pegged to the rate of inflation, the bonds offer investors a safer type of Treasury bond investment option. This portion of your return is reflected as an inflation adjustment to the principal you invested. The other portion of your return is paid out in interest. Thus, an inflation-indexed Treasury bond investor would not see the purchasing power of his investment eroded by unexpected inflation.

Inflation-indexed Treasuries can be a good investment for conservative, inflation-worried bond investors, as well as taxpayers who want to hold the government accountable for increases in inflation. The downside: Inflation-indexed bonds can yield slightly lower returns, because they're less risky compared to regular Treasury bonds.

 If you want a low-cost method of investing in Treasury bonds, you can purchase Treasuries directly from the Federal Reserve Bank. To open an account through the Treasury Direct program, call 800-722-2678, or visit the Web site at www.treasurydirect.gov.

You do sacrifice a bit of liquidity, however, when purchasing Treasury bonds directly from the government. You can sell your bonds prior to maturity through the Treasury (for a $45 fee), but it takes some time and hassle. If you want daily access to your money, buy a recommended Vanguard fund and pay the company's low management fee.

Purchasing certificates of deposit (CDs)

Bank CDs are popular with generally older, safety-minded investors with some extra cash that they don't need in the near future (typically a year or two). With a CD, you get a higher rate of return than you get on a bank savings account. And unlike with bond and stock funds, your principal doesn't fluctuate in value.

Compared to bonds, however, CDs have a couple of drawbacks:

- ✔ **Inaccessibility:** In a CD, your money isn't accessible unless you pay a penalty — typically six months' interest. With a no-load (commission-free) bond fund, you can access your money without penalty whenever you need it.

- ✔ **Taxability:** Interest from CDs is taxable. Bonds, on the other hand, come in tax-free (federal and/or state) and taxable flavors. So bonds offer higher-tax-bracket investors a tax-friendly option that CDs can't match.

 In the long run, you should earn more — perhaps 1 to 2 percent more per year — and have better access to your money in bond funds than in CDs. Bond funds make particular sense when you're in a higher tax bracket and you'd benefit from tax-free income on your investments (by investing in municipal bond funds). If you're not in a high tax bracket and you have a bad day whenever your bond fund takes a dip in value, consider CDs. Just make sure that you shop around to get the best interest rate.

Investing in stocks and stock funds

Stocks have stood the test of time for building wealth. (In Chapter 11, I discuss picking individual stocks versus investing through stock mutual funds.) Remember that when you invest in stocks in taxable (nonretirement) accounts, all the distributions on those stocks, such as dividends and capital gains, are taxable. Stock dividends and long-term capital gains do benefit from lower tax rates (maximum of 15 percent, but this may increase for higher income brackets because of possible Congressional action).

Some stock-picking advocates argue that you should shun stock funds because of tax considerations. I disagree. You can avoid stock funds that generate a lot of short-term capital gains, which are taxed at the relatively high ordinary income tax rates. *Index funds,* which invest in a fixed mix of stocks to track a particular market index, are tax-efficient. Additionally, some fund companies offer tax-friendly stock funds, which are appropriate if you don't want current income or you're in a high federal tax bracket and seek to minimize receiving taxable distributions on your funds.

 Vanguard (800-662-7447; www.vanguard.com) offers the best menu of tax-managed stock funds. Alternatively, you can invest in a wider variety of diversified stock funds inside an annuity (see the following section).

Checking out annuities

Annuities are accounts that are partly insurance but mostly investment. Consider contributing to an annuity only after you exhaust contributions to all your available retirement accounts. Because annuities carry higher annual operating expenses than comparable mutual funds, you should consider them only if you plan to leave your money invested, preferably for 15 years or more. Even if you leave your money invested for that long, tax-friendly funds can allow your money to grow without excessive annual taxation.

The best annuities can be purchased from no-load (commission-free) mutual fund companies — specifically Vanguard (800-662-7447; www.vanguard.com), Fidelity (800-544-4702; www.fidelity.com), and T. Rowe Price (800-638-5660; www.troweprice.com).

Investing Retirement Account Money

If you're in your 20s, the good news is that you likely have decades to grow your nest egg before you need to draw on the bulk of your retirement account assets. The more years you have before you're going to retire, the greater your ability to take risk. As long as the value of your investments has time to recover, what's the big deal if some of your investments drop a bit over a year or two? Of course, you should be concerned with growing your portfolio enough to keep you ahead of the inevitable inflation that occurs over the years.

 Think of your retirement accounts as part of your overall plan to generate retirement income. Then allocate different types of investments between your tax-advantaged retirement accounts and other taxable investment accounts to get the maximum benefit of tax deferral. This section helps you determine how to distribute your money in retirement plans.

Establishing and prioritizing retirement contributions

When you have access to various retirement accounts, prioritize which account you're going to use first by determining how much each gives you in return. You should focus your contributions in this order:

1. **First give to employer-based plans that match your contributions.**

2. **Next, contribute to any other employer or self-employed plans that allow tax-deductible contributions.**

3. **After you contribute as much as possible to these tax-deductible plans (or if you don't have access to such plans), contribute to an IRA.**

4. **If you max out on contributions to an IRA, exceed the income limitations for an IRA contribution, or don't have this choice because you lack employment income, consider a Roth 401k (employer-offered, after-tax contributions) or an annuity.**

Investments and account types are different issues. People sometimes get confused when discussing the investments they make in retirement accounts — especially people who have a retirement account, such as an IRA, at a bank. They don't realize that you can have your IRA at a variety of financial institutions (for example, a mutual fund company or brokerage firm). At each financial institution, you can choose among the firm's investment options for investing your IRA money.

No-load, or commission-free, mutual fund and discount brokerage firms are your best bets for establishing a retirement account (see Chapter 11 for more information on these accounts).

Allocating money in employer plans

In some company-sponsored plans, such as 401(k)s, you're limited to a short list of investment choices. I discuss typical investment options for 401(k) plans in order of increasing risk and, hence, likely return:

- ✔ **Money market:** Folks who are skittish about the stock and bond markets are attracted to money market and savings accounts because they can't drop in value. In the long run, you won't be doing yourself any favors. Trying to time your investments to attempt to catch the lows and avoid the peaks isn't possible (see Chapter 11).

- ✔ **Bond mutual funds:** Bond mutual funds invest in a mixture of typically high-quality bonds. Bonds pay a higher yield than money funds. Depending on whether your plan's option is a short-term, intermediate-term, or long-term fund (maybe you have more than one type), the bond fund's current yield is probably a percent or two higher than the money market fund's yield. Bond funds carry higher yields than money market funds, but they also carry greater risk, because their value can fall if interest rates increase. However, bonds tend to be more stable in value over the shorter term (such as a few years) than stocks. Aggressive, younger investors should keep a minimum amount of money in bond funds (see the asset allocation discussion in Chapter 11).

✔ **Guaranteed-investment contracts (GICs), also known as stable value funds:** Guaranteed-investment contracts are backed by an insurance company, and they typically quote you an interest rate a year in advance. The attraction of these investments is that your account value doesn't fluctuate (at least, not that you can see). In GICs, you pay for the peace of mind of a guaranteed return with lower than bond fund long-term returns. And GICs have another minor drawback: Insurance companies, unlike mutual funds, can and do fail, putting GIC investment dollars at risk. Some retirement plans have been burned by insurer failures.

✔ **Balanced mutual funds:** Balanced mutual funds invest primarily in a mixture of stocks and bonds. This one-stop-shopping concept offers broad diversification, makes investing easier, and smoothes out fluctuations in the value of your investments. Funds investing exclusively in stocks or in bonds make for a rougher ride.

✔ **Stock mutual funds:** Stock mutual funds invest in stocks, which often provide greater long-term growth potential but also wider fluctuations in value from year to year. Some companies offer a number of different stock funds, including funds that invest overseas. Unless you plan to borrow against your funds to purchase a home (if your plan allows), you should have plenty of stock funds.

✔ **Stock in your employer:** Some companies offer employees the option of investing in the company's stock. I generally suggest avoiding this option because your future income and other employee benefits are already riding on the company's success. If the company hits the skids, you may lose your job and your benefits. You certainly don't want the value of your retirement account to depend on the same factors. If you think strongly that your company has its act together and the stock is a good buy, investing a portion of your retirement account is fine — but no more than 25 percent. Some employers offer employees an option to buy company stock outside a tax-deferred retirement plan at a discount, sometimes as much as 15 percent, to its current market value. If your company offers a discount on its stock, consider taking advantage of it. When you sell the stock, you're usually able to lock in a profit over your purchase price.

Table 12-1 shows a couple of examples of how people in different employer plans may choose to allocate their 401(k) investments among the plan's investment options. See Chapter 11
for more background on asset allocation decisions.

Table 12-1	Allocating 401(k) Investments	
Type of Fund	25-Year-Old Aggressive Risk Investor	30-Year-Old Moderate Risk Investor
Bond fund	0%	40%
Balanced fund (50% stock/50% bond)	10%	0%
Larger company stock fund(s)	30–40%	20%
Smaller company stock fund(s)	25%	20%
International stock fund(s)	25–35%	20%

Designating money in plans you design

With self-employed plans (SEP-IRAs and Keoghs), certain
403(b) plans for nonprofit employees, and IRAs, you may
select the investment options as well as the allocation of
money among them. In the sections that follow, I give some
specific recipes that you may find useful for investing at some
of the premier investment companies.

To establish your retirement account at one of these firms,
dial the company's toll-free number, and ask the representative to mail you an account application for the type of account
(for example, SEP-IRA, 403(b), and so on) you want to set up.
You can also have the company mail you background information on specific mutual funds. Many investment firms provide
downloadable account applications, and may allow you to
complete the application online.

Vanguard: No-load leader

Vanguard (800-662-7447; www.vanguard.com) is a mutual
fund powerhouse and also operates a discount brokerage
division. It's the largest no-load fund company and consistently has the lowest operating expenses in the business.

Historically, Vanguard's funds have excellent performance when compared to those of its peers, especially among conservatively managed bond and stock funds.

For an aggressive portfolio (80 percent stocks, 20 percent bonds), try this:

- ✔ Vanguard Star (fund of funds) — 50 percent
- ✔ Vanguard Total Stock Market Index — 30 percent
- ✔ Vanguard Total International Stock Index — 20 percent

Or you can place 100 percent in Vanguard LifeStrategy Growth (fund of funds). Note that this portfolio places less money overseas than the preceding example.

Fidelity: Investment behemoth

Fidelity Investments (800-544-8888; www.fidelity.com) is the largest provider of mutual funds in terms of total assets, and it operates a discount brokerage division. However, some Fidelity funds assess sales charges (no such funds are recommended in the sections that follow).

For an aggressive portfolio (80 percent stocks, 20 percent bonds), try this:

- ✔ Fidelity Puritan (balanced fund) — 35 percent
- ✔ Fidelity Disciplined Equity — 25 percent
- ✔ Fidelity Low-Priced Stock — 20 percent
- ✔ Vanguard Total International Stock Index and/or Masters' Select International — 20 percent

Discount brokers

A *discount brokerage account* can allow you centralized, one-stop shopping and the ability to hold mutual funds from a variety of leading fund companies. Some funds are available without transaction fees, although you pay a small transaction fee to buy most of the better funds. The reason: The discounter is a middleman between you and the fund companies.

You have to weigh the convenience of being able to buy and hold funds from multiple fund companies in a single account versus the lower cost of buying funds directly from their providers. A $25 to $30 transaction fee can gobble a sizable chunk of what you have to invest, especially if you're investing smaller amounts.

Among brokerage firms or brokerage divisions of mutual fund companies, for breadth of fund offerings and competitive pricing, I like TD Ameritrade (800-934-4448; www.tdameritrade.com), T. Rowe Price (800-225-5132; www.troweprice.com), and Vanguard (800-992-8327; www.vanguard.com).

For an aggressive portfolio (80 percent stocks, 20 percent bonds), try this:

- ✔ Harbor Bond and/or Vanguard Total Bond Market Index — 20 percent

- ✔ Vanguard Total Stock Market Index and/or Dodge & Cox Stock — 50 percent

- ✔ Masters' Select International and/or Vanguard International Growth and/or Vanguard Total International Stock — 30 percent

Investing for Education

Whether you're about to begin a regular college investment plan or you've already started saving, your emotions may lead you astray. The hype about educational costs may scare you into taking a financially detrimental path. Quality education for your children doesn't have to, and probably won't, cost you as much as gargantuan projections suggest. In this section, I explain the inner workings of the financial aid system, help you gauge how much money you'll need, and discuss educational investment options.

Understanding the importance of applying for financial aid

Just as your child shouldn't choose a college based solely on whether he thinks he can get in, he shouldn't choose a college on the basis of whether you think you can afford it. Except for the affluent, who can pay for the full cost of college, everyone else should apply for financial aid. Some parents who don't think that they qualify for financial aid are pleasantly surprised to find that their children have access to loans as well as grants (which don't have to be repaid).

Completing the Free Application for Federal Student Aid (FAFSA) is the first step in the financial aid process. (See the form online at www.fafsa.ed.gov.) Some private colleges also require completing the Financial Aid Form (FAF), which asks for more information than the FAFSA. Some schools also supplement the FAFSA with PROFILE forms; these forms are mainly used by costly private schools to differentiate need among financial aid applicants. States have their own financial aid programs, so apply to these programs as well if your child plans to attend an in-state college.

The data you supply through student aid forms is run through a financial needs analysis, a standard methodology approved by the U.S. Congress. The analysis calculates how much money you, as the parent(s), and your child, as the student, are expected to contribute toward educational expenses. Even if the needs analysis determines that you don't qualify for needs-based financial aid, you may still have access to loans that are not based on need. So be sure that you apply for financial aid.

Using your retirement accounts

Under the current financial needs analysis, the value of your retirement plans isn't considered an asset. By contrast, money that you save outside retirement accounts, especially money in the child's name, is counted as an asset and reduces your eligibility for financial aid.

Fund your retirement accounts, such as 401(k)s, SEP-IRAs, and Keogh plans. In addition to getting an immediate tax deduction on your contributions, future growth on your earnings grow without taxation while you're maximizing your child's chances of qualifying for aid. Forgoing contributions to your retirement savings plans to save in a taxable account for your kid's college fund is foolish because you'll be expected to contribute more to your child's educational costs.

Putting money in kids' names

Save money in your name rather than in your children's names if you plan to apply for financial aid. Colleges expect a much greater percentage of the money in your children's names to be used for college costs than the money in your name.

However, if you're affluent enough to foot your child's college bill without outside help, investing in your kid's name can save you money in taxes. Prior to your child's reaching age 18, the first $950 for 2010 of interest and dividend income is tax-free; the next $950 is taxed at 10 percent. Any income above $1,900 is taxed at the parents' marginal tax rate. Upon reaching age 19 (or age 24 if your offspring are still full-time students), income generated by investments in your child's name is taxed at your child's presumably lower tax rate. Parents control a custodial account until the child reaches either the age of 18 or 21, depending on the state in which you reside.

Tapping into Education Savings Accounts

Education Savings Accounts (ESAs) are another option that, like a traditional custodial account, makes sense for affluent parents who don't expect to apply for or need any type of financial aid. As with regular custodial accounts, parents who have their kids apply for financial aid will be penalized by college financial aid offices for having ESA balances.

Subject to eligibility requirements, you can put up to $2,000 per child per year into an ESA. Single taxpayers with adjusted gross incomes (AGIs) of $110,000 or more and couples with AGIs of $220,000 or more may not contribute to an ESA (although another individual, such as a grandparent, may make the contribution to the child's account). Although the contribution isn't tax-deductible, future investment earnings compound without taxation. Upon withdrawal, the investment earnings aren't taxed as long as the money is used for qualified education expenses.

Using 529 college savings plans

Section 529 plans are named after Internal Revenue Code Section 529 and also known as qualified state tuition plans. A parent or grandparent can generally put more than $200,000 per beneficiary into one of these plans.

The attraction of the Section 529 plans is that money inside the plans compounds without tax, and if it's used to pay for college tuition, room and board, and other related higher-education expenses, the investment earnings and appreciation can be withdrawn tax-free. In addition to paying college costs, the money in Section 529 plans may also be used for graduate school expenses. Some states provide additional tax benefits on contributions to their state-sanctioned plan.

You can generally invest in any state plan to pay college expenses in any state, regardless of where you live.

A big potential drawback of the Section 529 plans — especially for families hoping for some financial aid — is that college financial aid offices treat assets in these plans as parental nonretirement assets. Even worse, the assets can be considered as belonging to an older child when an independent young adult no longer reports parental financial information for financial aid purposes.

Please also be aware that a future Congress could change the tax laws affecting these plans, diminishing the tax breaks or increasing the penalties for nonqualified withdrawals.

529 plans make sense for affluent parents (or grandparents) to establish for children who don't expect to qualify for financial aid. Do your research and homework before investing in any plan. Check out the investment track record and fees in each plan, as well as restrictions on transferring to other plans or changing beneficiaries. See my Web site (`www.erictyson.com`) for more information on these plans.

Treating home equity and other assets

Your family's assets may also include equity in real estate and businesses that you own. Although the federal financial aid analysis no longer counts equity in your primary residence as an asset, many private (independent) schools continue to ask parents for this information when making their own financial aid determinations. Therefore, paying down your home mortgage more quickly instead of funding retirement accounts can harm you financially: You may end up with less financial aid and a higher tax bill.

Paying for educational costs

Although you may not have children yet or your children are young, you've probably started thinking about how you're going to pay for their college expenses. College can cost a lot. The total costs, including tuition, fees, books, supplies, room, board, and transportation, vary substantially from school to school. The total average annual cost is running around $40,000 per year at private colleges and around $20,000 (in-state rate) at public colleges. Figuring out how you're going to pay these expenses can be overwhelming.

You first want to put as much money as possible in your retirement accounts. If you have money left over after taking advantage of retirement accounts, try to save for your children's college costs. Save in your name unless you know that you aren't going to apply for financial aid, including those loans that are available regardless of your economic situation.

Be realistic about what you can afford for college expenses given your other financial goals. Being able to personally pay 100 percent of the cost of a college education, especially at a four-year private college, is a luxury of the affluent. If you're not a high-income earner, consider trying to save enough to pay a third or, at most, half of the cost. You can make up the balance through a wide variety of means, such as the following:

✔ **Loans:** A host of financial aid programs, including a number of loan programs, allow you to borrow at reasonable interest rates. Federal government educational loans have variable interest rates, which means that the interest rate you're charged floats, or varies, with the overall level of interest rates. The rates are also capped so that the rate can never exceed several percent more than the initial rate on the loan.

A number of loan programs, such as unsubsidized Stafford Loans and Parent Loans for Undergraduate Students (PLUS), are available even when your family is not deemed financially needy. Only subsidized Stafford Loans, on which the federal government pays the interest that accumulates while the student is still in school, are limited to students deemed financially needy. For more information about these loan programs, call the Federal Student Aid Information Center at 800-433-3243 or visit their Web site at www.studentaid.ed.gov.

✔ **Grants:** In addition to loans, a number of grant programs are available through schools, the government, and independent sources. You can apply for federal government grants via the FAFSA. Grants available through state government programs may require a separate application. Specific colleges and other private organizations (for example, employers, banks, credit unions, and community groups) also offer grants and scholarships.

✔ **Your home's equity:** If you're a homeowner, you may be able to borrow against the *equity* (market value less the outstanding mortgage loan) in your property. This option is useful because you can borrow against your home at a reasonable interest rate, and the interest is generally tax-deductible. Some company retirement plans, such as 401(k)s, allow borrowing as well.

✔ **IRAs:** Parents may make penalty-free withdrawals from individual retirement accounts if the funds are used for college expenses. Although you won't be charged an early-withdrawal penalty, the IRS (and most states) will treat the amount withdrawn as taxable income. On top of that, the financial aid office will look at your beefed-up income and assume that you don't need as much financial aid. (You can make qualified withdrawals from Roth IRAs and not be taxed.)

✔ **Your child's employment:** Your child can work during the summer and save that money for educational expenses. Besides giving your child a stake in his own future, this training encourages sound personal financial management.

Part IV

Insurance: You're Not as Invincible or Independent as You Think!

The 5th Wave — By Rich Tennant

"You put in your height, weight, and marital status here. At the end of your workout, it shows your heart rate, blood pressure, and the type of insurance you should be carrying."

In this part . . .

I discuss protecting yourself with cost-effective insurance. When you're young and healthy, it's easy to ignore the chances that your life could change. But you should have health insurance to protect against large medical expenses, and you should also protect your income against disability. If you have financial dependents, you may also need some life insurance. Finally, I discuss auto, renters, and other policies you may or may not need.

Chapter 13

The Lowdown on Health Insurance

*W*hen you're young and living under your parents' roof, you're unlikely to be concerned with health insurance. School-aged kids generally get their health insurance through a parent's coverage, a practice that's usually continued through college.

Reality and awareness of health insurance for adult children in their 20s often sets in when parents realize that their offspring are about to lose their coverage either because their now-adult child has graduated or has reached a certain age (for example, 25) that triggers the insurance company to discontinue coverage.

Welcome to the adult world of insurance and, more specifically, health insurance! Health insurance was in the news soon after the election of President Barack Obama because he promised during the campaign, and then pushed for a national health insurance program mandated by the federal government. In this chapter, I discuss the best and most affordable ways to secure health insurance in your 20s as well as the ramifications of the healthcare bill that was signed into law in 2010.

Making Sure That You're Covered

Having health insurance is essential for nearly everyone, no matter your age. Many people get health insurance through their employers. Unfortunately, plenty of people don't have coverage. In fact, studies estimate that about one in five folks in their 20s lack health insurance coverage.

Some people who can afford health insurance choose not to buy it because they believe that they're healthy and they're not going to need it. Others who opt not to buy health insurance figure that if they ever really need healthcare, they'll get it even if they can't fully afford it.

Although you may think you're healthy and don't need health insurance, think again. People without health insurance are more prone to put off getting routine care, which can lead to small problems turning into big ones. Besides this being an unwise approach to optimizing your health, it probably costs more because of advanced illness, emergency room visits, and so on.

The good news: Getting coverage in your 20s is easier now with the 2010 healthcare laws that make some significant changes affecting access to health insurance. This section discusses transitioning from your parents' coverage to your own and how the healthcare laws help you get coverage.

Transitioning your coverage

Each state has its own laws as far as health insurance coverage goes, so there's no one-size-fits-all approach. In most states, an adult child generally loses health insurance coverage under a parent's policy upon college graduation or when turning a particular age (for example, 25 or 26). But each state has a unique set of laws. Consider, for example, three state rules I pulled at random:

  ✔ Connecticut requires that group comprehensive and health insurance policies extend coverage to unwed children until the age of 26, provided they remain residents of Connecticut or are full-time students.

✔ Florida allows for dependent children up to age 25 who live with a parent or are students, and those up to 30 who are also unmarried and have no dependent children of their own, to remain on their parents' insurance.

✔ Wyoming allows a child who's unmarried and a full-time student to remain on a parent's insurance up to age 23 if the parent is covered by a small, group policy.

What a headache! So what are the best ways to negotiate keeping health insurance coverage in your 20s without spending a small fortune for coverage? Here's my advice:

✔ **Consider staying on your parents' policy until you secure full-time employment.** As soon as you're eligible for your employer's health plan, sign up for it.

✔ **If you don't have access to your own coverage through your employer, look to COBRA.** The Consolidated Omnibus Budget Reconciliation Act (COBRA) enables you to stay on your parents' policy for up to 36 months from the time you lose coverage on that policy. Just be aware that you have to pay the full premiums.

✔ **If you're self-employed, or your employer doesn't offer health coverage, or the coverage isn't very good, get your own policy with a high deductible.** A *deductible* is the amount of medical claims you must first pay out of your pocket before insurance coverage kicks in. Check out the later section "Finding Your Best Health Plan" for advice. You can then sock money away in a health savings account (HSA) if you desire. See the section on HSAs later in this chapter.

Seeing how the 2010 healthcare laws make coverage easier

In 2010, Congress passed, and President Obama signed, two comprehensive healthcare reform bills that affect how you can get health insurance coverage. Summarizing thousands of pages of legislation in a concise space is challenging, but the reality is that the highlights that apply to individuals in their 20s aren't that extensive.

Effective 2010, the following applies to group health plans offered through employers:

- ✔ They must offer coverage to their employees for their adult children up to age 26 who aren't eligible for coverage under another employer's health plan. So if your mother or father is covered under a group health plan, you may get coverage through that plan through age 26, even if you aren't a dependent for income tax purposes. The coverage isn't taxable to the employee or dependent.

- ✔ They may not impose lifetime limits on claims paid (annual limits are prohibited effective 2014).

- ✔ They may not exclude children under 19 for preexisting conditions.

Higher-income earners will be subjected to some higher taxes effective 2013 to help pay for the health bill:

- ✔ Single taxpayers with earned income above $200,000 and married couples filing jointly with earned income above $250,000 will pay an extra 0.9 percent Medicare tax on wages and self-employment income in excess of these thresholds.

- ✔ Taxpayers with modified adjusted income (MAGI) from any source (including investments) above these thresholds will be subject to a 3.8 percent tax on the lesser of their net investment income (for example, interest, dividends, and capital gains) and the amount by which their modified adjusted gross income exceeds the thresholds.

By 2014, the following noteworthy changes become effective:

- ✔ Employers must offer minimum coverage to full-time employees or make payments to the government.

- ✔ Group health plans must limit cost sharing and deductibles to those in a health savings account–eligible, high-deductible health plan.

- ✔ Group health plans must remove all preexisting condition exclusions on all participants.

- ✔ An individual health coverage mandate begins with certain exceptions. Individuals who don't enroll in minimum essential coverage would pay a penalty based on the greater of a flat dollar amount or a percentage of income. *Minimum essential coverage* includes Medicare, Medicaid, employer plans, and exchange-based (government-sanctioned) health coverage. The annual flat dollar penalty would equal $95 in 2014, $325 in 2015, and $695 in 2016, and then it would be indexed to changes in the cost of living thereafter. The percentage of income would equal 1 percent in 2014, 2 percent in 2015, and 2.5 percent in 2016 and subsequent years. The penalty would be 50 percent of these amounts for those under age 18 who don't maintain health coverage. Individuals with income below the tax-filing threshold won't pay the assessment (for example, a married couple with income below $18,700).

Finding Your Best Health Plan

Most working-age folks obtain health insurance through their employer. Employer-provided coverage eliminates the hassle of your having to shop for coverage from scratch. Also, employer-provided coverage usually provides a higher level of benefits, given the cost, than individually purchased coverage.

If you're self-employed, out of work, or working for an employer that doesn't offer health coverage, you need to shop for and secure health insurance. And even if your employer does offer health policies, you may well have choices to make. In the following sections, I discuss the important issues to consider when selecting among available health insurance plans.

Selection of doctors and hospitals

Open-choice plans that allow you to use any doctor or hospital you want are less common and generally more expensive than *restricted-choice plans,* such as *health maintenance organizations* (HMOs) and *preferred provider organizations* (PPOs). These plans keep costs down because they negotiate low rates with selected providers.

HMOs and PPOs are more similar than they are different. The main difference is that PPOs still pay the majority of your expenses if you use a provider outside their approved list. If you use a provider outside the approved list with an HMO, you typically aren't covered at all.

If you want to use particular doctors or hospitals, find out which health insurance plans they accept as payment. Weigh whether the extra cost of an open-choice plan is worth being able to use the services of particular medical providers if they're not part of a restricted-choice plan. Also be aware that some plans allow you to go outside their network of providers as long as you pay a bigger portion of the incurred medical costs. If you're interested in using alternative types of providers, such as acupuncturists, find out whether the plans you're considering cover these services.

Plan benefits and features

Healthcare plans typically offer many bells and whistles. The following identifies the key features to search for to ensure a quality plan at the most reasonable cost:

- ✔ **Major medical coverage:** This includes hospital care, physician visits, and ancillary charges, such as X-rays and laboratory work. If you're a woman and you think you may want to have children, make sure that your plan has maternity benefits.

- ✔ **Deductibles and co-payments:** To reduce your health insurance premiums, choose a plan with the highest deductible and *co-payment* (the amount you pay when service is rendered, such as $10 to $30) you can afford. As with other insurance policies, the more you're willing to share in the cost of your claims, the less you'll have to pay in premiums. Most policies have annual deductible options (usually $250, $500, or $1,000) as well as co-payment options, which are typically 20 percent or so of the claim amount. Insurance plans generally set a maximum out-of-pocket limit such as $1,000 or $2,000 on your annual co-payments. The insurer covers 100 percent of any medical expenses that go over that cap. Most HMO plans don't have deductible and co-payment options.

If you have existing health problems and you're in a group plan through your employer, consider plans with low out-of-pocket expenses. Because you're part of a group, the insurer won't increase your individual rates just because you file more claims.

✔ **Lifetime maximum benefits:** Health insurance plans specify the maximum total benefits they'll pay over the course of time you're insured by their plan. With the high cost of healthcare, you should choose a plan that has no maximum or that has a maximum of at least $5 million. In future years, the national health insurance bill signed into law in 2010 prevents insurers from setting lifetime maximums. See the section "Seeing how the 2010 healthcare laws make coverage easier" earlier in this chapter.

Shopping for Health Insurance

Yes, health insurance is among the more complicated things to shop for, but it's like other products and services — there's a marketplace of providers competing for your business. This section explains how to unearth your best options and what to do in case you're denied coverage.

Uncovering the best policies

When shopping for health insurance, you basically have two options: You can buy a health plan through an agent or you can buy directly from an insurer. When health insurance is sold both ways, buying through an agent usually doesn't cost more.

If you're self-employed or you work for a smaller employer that doesn't offer health insurance as a benefit, get proposals from the larger and older health insurers in your area. Larger plans can negotiate better rates from providers, and older plans are more likely to be here tomorrow. Nationally, Blue Cross Blue Shield, Kaiser Permanente, Aetna, UnitedHealth Group, CIGNA, Assurant, Golden Rule, and Anthem are among the older and bigger health insurers.

Many insurers operate in a bunch of different insurance businesses. You want an insurer that's one of the biggest in the health insurance arena and is committed to that business. If your coverage is canceled, you may have to search for coverage that allows an existing medical problem, and other health insurers may not want to insure you. (Find out whether your state department of insurance offers a plan for people unable to get coverage; check out the next section for more info.)

Also check with professional or other associations that you belong to, as such plans sometimes offer decent benefits at a competitive price because of the purchasing clout they possess. A competent independent insurance agent who specializes in health insurance can help you find insurers who are willing to offer you coverage.

Health insurance agents have a conflict of interest that's common to all financial salespeople who work on commission: The higher the premium plan they sell you, the bigger the commission they earn. So an agent may try to steer you into higher-cost plans and avoid suggesting some of the cost-reducing strategies that I discuss in this chapter, such as opting for a higher deductible.

Handling rejection

When you try to enroll in a particular health insurance plan, you may be turned down because of current or previous health problems. Here are strategies to find out why and finally get approved:

- ✔ **Ask the insurer why you were denied.** If you're denied coverage because of a medical condition, find out what information the company has and determine whether it's accurate. Perhaps the company made a mistake or misinterpreted some information that you provided in your application.

- ✔ **Request a copy of your medical information file.** Just as you have a credit report file that details your use (and misuse) of credit (see Chapter 6), you also have a medical information report. Once per year, you can request a free copy of your medical information file (which typically highlights only the more significant problems over the past seven years, not your entire medical history) by calling 866-692-6901 or visiting www.mib.com (click the "Consumers" tab and then the link "Request Your MIB Consumer File"). If you find a mistake on your report, you have the right to request that it be fixed. However, the burden is on you to prove that the information in your file is incorrect. Proving that your file contains errors can be a major hassle — you may even need to contact physicians you saw in the past because their medical records may be the source of the incorrect information.

✔ **Shop around.** Just because one company denies you coverage doesn't mean that all insurance companies will deny you. Some insurers better understand certain medical conditions and are more comfortable accepting applicants with those conditions. Although most insurers charge higher rates to people with blemished medical histories than people with perfect health records, some companies penalize them less than others. An agent who sells policies from multiple insurers, called an *independent agent,* can be helpful because she can shop among a number of different companies.

✔ **If you have a preexisting condition (current or prior medical problems), find a job with an employer whose health insurer doesn't require a medical exam.** Of course, this shouldn't be your only reason for seeking new employment, but it can be an important factor. If you're married, you may also be able to get into an employer group plan if your spouse takes a new job.

✔ **Find out about state high-risk pools.** A number of states act as the insurer of last resort and provide insurance for those who can't get it from insurance companies. State high-risk pool coverage is usually quite basic, but it beats going without any coverage. The Health Insurance Resource Center Web site provides links to all state health coverage high-risk pool Web sites at `www.health insurance.org/risk_pools/`. Alternatively, you can check with your state department of insurance (see the "Government" section of your local white pages) for high-risk pools for other types of insurance, such as property coverage.

Health Savings Accounts: Tax Reduction for Healthcare Costs

Health savings accounts (HSAs) are terrific for reducing your taxes while saving money for healthcare expenses. They especially make sense if you're self-employed or an employee of a smaller company with no health plan or a high-deductible health plan.

An HSA is fairly simple: You put money earmarked for medical expenses into an investment account that offers tax-deductible contributions and tax-deferred compounding, just like a retirement account (withdrawals aren't taxed so long as the money is used for qualified healthcare expenses). For tax year 2011, you can sock away up to $3,050 for an individual account and $6,150 for a family account. To qualify for an HSA, you must have a high-deductible health insurance policy — at least $1,200 for individuals and $2,400 for families.

You don't have to deplete the HSA by the end of the year: Money can compound tax-deferred inside the HSA for years. If you qualify, you can begin to investigate an HSA through insurers offering health plans you're interested in or with the company you currently have coverage through (also see my Web site, www.erictyson.com, for the latest information on the best HSAs).

You may also be able to save on taxes if you have a substantial amount of healthcare expenditures in a year relative to your income. You can deduct medical and dental expenses as an itemized deduction on Schedule A to the extent that they exceed 7.5 percent of your adjusted gross income.

If you expect to have out-of-pocket medical expenses and can't qualify for an HSA because of your employer's plans, find out whether your employer offers a *flexible spending* or *healthcare reimbursement account.* These accounts enable you to pay for uncovered medical expenses with pretax dollars. If, for example, you're in a combined 35 percent federal and state income tax bracket, these accounts allow you to pay for necessary healthcare at a 35 percent discount. These accounts can also be used to pay for vision and dental care.

Be forewarned of the major stumbling blocks you face when saving through medical reimbursement accounts:

- ✔ **You need to elect to save money from your paycheck prior to the beginning of each plan year.** The only exception is at the time of a "life change," such as marriage, a spouse's job change, divorce, the birth of a child, or a family member's death.

- ✔ **You also need to use the money within the year you save it.** These accounts contain a "use it or lose it" feature.

Chapter 14

Safeguarding Your Income

● ●

In This Chapter

▶ Dissecting the ins and outs of disability coverage

▶ Figuring out the fine points of life insurance

▶ Taking time to get your affairs in order for loved ones

● ●

*I*f you're like most folks in their 20s and in good health, you probably don't think much about possible health changes. But you need to take the right steps to make sure that you protect your primary source of income in case of an unexpected health problem.

If you earn income from working, you probably need some insurance to protect that stream of income, not only for yourself but also possibly for loved ones if they're dependent on you financially. In this chapter, I discuss the two forms of insurance — disability and life insurance — that can help you address these needs. I also discuss other simple yet powerful steps beyond insurance that you can take to get things in order for your loved ones.

Protecting Your Income for You and Yours: Disability Insurance

Disability insurance protects your income for yourself and perhaps also for your dependents. But even if no one depends on you financially, you need long-term disability insurance if you depend on your own income. After all, if you become disabled, you probably won't be able to earn employment income, but your living expenses will continue. And therein lies the need for disability insurance.

When you're young and healthy, dismissing the need for disability insurance is easy because the odds of suffering a long-term disability seem — and are — relatively low. But the occurrence of a long-term disability is unpredictable, and plenty of long-term disabilities affect younger people. Some disabilities happen because of accidents, and those can happen to you regardless of age. Others are caused by medical problems, and more than one-third of all such disabilities are suffered by people under the age of 45. The vast majority of these medical problems can't be predicted in advance.

In the following sections, I assist you with understanding what coverage you may already have and determining whether you need disability insurance, how much to get, what features to seek in a policy, and where to actually buy a policy.

Understanding disability coverage you may already have

Through payroll-deduction payment of taxes, you may have some disability coverage through state and federal government insurance programs. However, this coverage is more short term than long term in nature:

- ✓ **State disability programs:** Some states have disability insurance programs, but the coverage is typically Spartan. Benefits are paid over a short period of time (usually one year at most). State programs are also generally not a good value because of the cost for the small amount of coverage they provide.

- ✓ **Social Security disability:** Social Security pays long-term benefits only if you're unable to perform any substantial, gainful activity for more than a year or if your disability is expected to result in death. Furthermore, Social Security disability payments are quite low because they're intended to provide only for basic, subsistence-level living expenses. Also, because you've only been working for a short amount of time, you haven't paid much into Social Security and thus won't have a high level of earned benefits.

What about coverage you have through your employer? If you're self-employed or work for a small company, you probably don't have long-term disability coverage. By contrast, most large employers offer disability insurance to their employees. Ask your employer's benefits department for details on your current policy and then compare those with the features that I recommend you get on a policy that you buy for yourself.

Workers' compensation, if you have such coverage through your employer, pays out if you're injured on the job, but it doesn't pay any benefits if you get disabled away from your job. You need coverage that pays no matter where and how you're disabled.

Determining your need for disability coverage

You should carry sufficient long-term disability insurance coverage to provide you with income to live on should you become disabled. If you don't have many financial assets and you want to maintain your current lifestyle if you suffer a disability, get enough coverage to replace your entire monthly take-home (after-tax) pay.

The benefits you purchase on a disability policy are quoted as the dollars per month you receive if disabled. So if your job provides you with a $3,000-per-month income after taxes, get a policy that provides a $3,000-per-month benefit.

If you pay for your disability insurance, the benefits are tax-free (but hopefully you won't ever have to collect them). If your employer picks up the tab, your benefits are taxable, so you need a greater amount of benefits.

In addition to the monthly coverage amount, you also need to select the duration for which you want a policy to pay you benefits. You should select a policy that pays benefits until you reach an age at which you become financially self-sufficient. For most people, that's around the age when their Social Security benefits kick in. (Folks born after 1959 get full Social Security benefits at age 67 and reduced benefits before that age.)

Identifying useful disability policy features

If you go shopping for a long-term disability (LTD) insurance policy, you need to master some jargon. LTD policies have plenty of features, some of which you need and some of which you don't. Here's what you need to know:

- **Definition of disability:** An *own-occupation* disability policy provides benefit payments if you can't perform the work you normally do. The extra cost of such policies is worthwhile if you're in a high-income or specialized occupation and you'd have to take a significant pay cut to do something else (and the reduced income and required lifestyle changes wouldn't be acceptable to you). Other policies pay you only if you're unable to perform a job for which you're reasonably trained.

- **Noncancelable and guaranteed renewable:** These desirable features ensure that your policy can't be canceled because of your developing health problems.

- **Waiting period:** The lag time between the onset of your disability and the time you begin collecting benefits is a disability policy's *deductible.*

    As with other types of insurance, you should take the highest deductible (longest waiting period) that your financial circumstances allow. A longer waiting period significantly reduces the policy's cost. The minimum waiting period on most policies is 30 days. The maximum waiting period can be up to one to two years. Try a waiting period of three to six months if you have sufficient emergency reserves.

- **Residual benefits:** This useful option pays you a partial benefit if you have a disability that prevents you from working full time.

- **Cost-of-living adjustments (COLAs):** This feature automatically increases your benefit payment by a set percentage annually or in accordance with changes in inflation. The advantage of a COLA is that it retains the purchasing power of your benefits. A modest COLA, such as 3 percent, is worth having.

✔ **Future insurability:** This allows you, regardless of health, to buy additional coverage in the future. You may benefit from the future insurability option if your income is artificially low now and your career trajectory suggests that your income will rise significantly in the future.

✔ **Insurer's financial stability:** Choose insurers that will be here tomorrow to pay your claim. But don't obsess over the company's stability; benefits are paid even if an insurer fails, because the state or another insurer almost always bails out the unstable insurer.

Shopping for coverage

When you start to shop for LTD, focus your attention first on group plans, which generally offer the best value. You may have access to buy group disability insurance through your employer or a professional association. Just be sure that the group plan policy includes the features I discuss in the preceding section.

If you don't have access to a group policy, you'll likely end up buying an individual policy through an agent. Some agents are called *independent agents* because they sell policies from numerous insurance companies. Other agents are dedicated to selling policies from a single company. Both types are fine to use so long as you shop the marketplace and get a policy with the features that I recommend in the preceding section.

Tread carefully when purchasing disability insurance through an agent. Some agents try to load your policy with all sorts of extra bells and whistles to pump up the premium — along with their commission.

Protecting Your Income for Dependents: Life Insurance

You generally need life insurance when others, such as a spouse or a child, depend on your income, especially if you have major financial commitments such as a mortgage or years of child rearing ahead. You may also want to consider life insurance if an extended family member currently depends on your income, or is likely to do so in the future.

You generally don't need life insurance if you're

- ✔ Single with no children
- ✔ Part of a working couple that can maintain an acceptable lifestyle on one of your incomes
- ✔ Independently wealthy and don't need to work

These sections explain how to figure out how much life insurance coverage you may already have, how much you need, and how to purchase it.

Assessing your current life insurance coverage

In a moment, I discuss how much coverage you may need if you've decided you need life insurance protection. First, though, you should inventory your current coverage. Start with your current employer and determine whether the company offers you any life insurance coverage at its own expense.

Next, consider possible coverage you may have through Social Security that provides survivor's benefits to your spouse and children. Be aware, however, that if your surviving spouse works and earns even a modest amount of money, he or she will get little, if any, survivor's benefits. Prior to reaching Social Security's full retirement age (67 for those born after 1959), your survivor's benefits get reduced by $1 for every $2 you earn above $14,160 (in 2010).

You should receive an annual estimate of your Social Security benefits after you have some work history. If you haven't received one in a while, complete Form 7004 from the Social Security Administration (800-772-1213; www.ssa.gov) for an estimate of your Social Security benefits. If either you or your spouse anticipates earning a low enough income to qualify for survivor's benefits, you should factor those benefits into how much life insurance to buy. For example, if your annual after-tax income is $30,000 and Social Security provides a survivor's benefit of $10,000 annually, you'd need enough life insurance to replace $20,000 annually ($30,000 – $10,000).

Determining how much life insurance to buy

To figure the amount of life insurance to buy, ask yourself how many years of income you want to replace. Table 14-1 provides a simple way to calculate how much life insurance you need to consider purchasing. To replace a certain number of years' worth of income, multiply the appropriate number in the table by your annual after-tax income. Because life insurance policy payouts aren't taxed, you need to replace only after-tax income and not pre-tax income.

Table 14-1	Figuring Life Insurance Needs
To Replace This Many Years of Income	*Multiply Your Annual After-Tax Income By*
5	4.5
10	8.5
20	15
30	20

You can figure your annual after-tax income in one of two ways. You can calculate it by getting out last year's tax return (and Form W-2) and subtracting the federal, state, and Social Security taxes you paid from your gross employment income. Alternatively, you can estimate your annual after-tax income by multiplying your gross income by 80 percent if you're a low-income earner, 70 percent if you're a moderate-income earner, or 60 percent if you're a high-income earner.

Deciding what type of life insurance to buy

Before you purchase any life insurance, you need to know your options. Life insurance comes in two major types:

> ✔ **Term insurance:** You pay an annual premium (as you do for your auto insurance), for which you receive a particular amount of life insurance protection. If you die during

> the term, your beneficiaries collect; otherwise, the premium is gone but you're grateful to be alive!
>
> ✔ **Cash value insurance:** All other life insurance policies (whole, universal, variable, and so on) combine life insurance with a supposed savings feature. A portion of your premiums is credited to an investment account that grows in value over time.

Purchase low-cost term insurance and do your investing separately. Life insurance is rarely a permanent need; over time, you can reduce the amount of term insurance you carry as your financial obligations lessen and you accumulate more assets. Cash value life insurance makes sense for some people, such as small-business owners who own a business worth at least several million dollars and who don't want their heirs to be forced to sell the business to pay estate taxes in the event of their death.

Insurance salespeople aggressively push cash value policies because of the high commissions that insurance companies pay them. That's why these policies explicitly penalize you for withdrawing your cash balance within the first seven to ten years. You're paying for these high commissions when you buy one of these policies. Also, you're more likely to buy less life insurance coverage than you need because of the high cost of cash value policies relative to the cost of term. The vast majority of life insurance buyers need more protection than they can afford to buy with cash value coverage.

Shopping for life insurance

You can purchase term life insurance so that your premium increases annually or it increases after 5, 10, 15, 20, or 30 years. The advantage of a premium that locks in for, say, 20 years is that you have the security of knowing how much you'll be paying each year for the next two decades. You also don't need to go through medical evaluations as frequently to qualify for the lowest rate possible.

The disadvantage of a policy with a long-term rate lock is that you pay more in the early years than you do on a policy that adjusts more frequently. In addition, you may want to change the amount of insurance you carry as your circumstances change. Thus, you may throw money away when you dump a policy with a long-term premium guarantee before its rate is set to change. Policies that adjust the premium every five to ten years offer a balance between price and predictability.

 Be sure to get a policy that's *guaranteed renewable,* which assures that the policy can't be canceled because of your health worsening. Don't buy a life insurance policy without this feature unless you expect that your life insurance needs will disappear when the policy is up for renewal.

Here are some sources for high-quality, low-cost term insurance (the first three are independent agencies):

- ✔ AccuQuote: www.accuquote.com; 800-442-9899
- ✔ ReliaQuote: www.reliaquote.com; 800-940-3002
- ✔ SelectQuote: www.selectquote.com; 800-963-8688
- ✔ Term4Sale: www.term4sale.com; 888-798-3488 (this company refers you to agents who sell life insurance)
- ✔ USAA: www.usaa.com; 800-531-8722 (this company sells low-cost term insurance directly to the public)

Caring for Your Loved Ones: "Peace of Mind" Insurance

Buying an insurance policy isn't the only thing you should do to provide for your loved ones. Consider taking the following steps, most of which involve only your time and forethought and no expense:

- ✔ **Centralize your important financial documents.** Keep your most recent investment account statements, insurance policies, employee benefits materials, small-business accounting records, and other important documents in one place (such as a file drawer) that your loved ones know about.
- ✔ **Prepare an up-to-date will.** You can do this yourself with a good software package such as those made by Nolo Press (www.nolo.com).

✔ **Provide a list of key contacts.** This list includes experts you recommend calling (or material you recommend reading) in the event of legal, financial, or tax quandaries.

✔ **Prepare sentimental remembrances.** You may want to give some thought to sentimental leave-behinds for your loved ones, especially for kids. These can be something like a short note telling them how much they meant to you and what you'd like them to remember about you.

Chapter 15

Home, Auto, Renters, and Other Insurance Policies

· ·

In This Chapter

▶ Insuring your home or rental property

▶ Protecting your car

▶ Knowing which coverages to skip

· ·

*N*o one likes to pay his hard-earned money to an insurance company. But if you wreck your car or someone breaks into your home and steals some valuable personal property, you'd be mighty unhappy if you lacked coverage and had to replace those items out of your own pocket.

So I understand that reading this chapter isn't on your short list of fun things to do today. But I do promise to clearly explain how to get the insurance protection you need on your property and personal possessions and to do so for the best price that you can. I also discuss smaller-type insurance policies that are likely to be a waste of your money and thus are best avoided.

Protecting Your Home and Possessions

After you buy a home (typically with a mortgage), the mortgage lender mandates that you get homeowners insurance. The lender wants to protect its investment in the property for the same reason that you should want to protect your stake in the property. This kind of policy insures your personal property and also provides some liability protection should a lawsuit arise out of something that happens at the property (an accident, for example).

If you're still renting, you should look into coverage for these same reasons — personal property coverage and liability protection.

Although homeowners insurance and renters insurance are completely separate policies, they share many important features, which I discuss in the following sections.

Dwelling coverage

When you buy a home, you'll get a policy with *dwelling protection,* the amount of which is determined by the cost of rebuilding in your area. The insurer details the size and features of your home so that, for example, in the event of a fire that destroys the property, you'd have enough money to rebuild the property and match what you started with. (As a condominium owner, check out whether the insurance the condo association bought for the entire building is sufficient.)

When buying a homeowners policy, seek out coverage that includes "guaranteed replacement cost." This ensures that the insurance company will rebuild the home even if the cost of construction is more than the policy coverage. If the insurance company underestimates your dwelling coverage, it has to make up the difference. Each insurer defines guaranteed replacement cost differently, so be sure to ask insurers how they define it. Some companies pay for the home's full replacement cost, no matter how much it ends up being, while other insurers set caps or limits. For example, some insurers may pay up to only 25 percent more than the dwelling coverage on your policy.

When you're renting, you don't need to have dwelling protection because you don't have an ownership stake in the building. Should something happen to the building, it could, of course, affect your ability to live there or affect your possessions, but those are different matters not covered by dwelling coverage, which is strictly for the building's owner.

Personal property protection

Personal property coverage basically covers the contents of your home — furniture, clothing, and other possessions. On a homeowners policy, the amount of personal property coverage is usually dictated by the amount of dwelling coverage. For example, you may get personal property coverage that's equal to 50 to 75 percent of the dwelling coverage, which should be more than enough for most people.

When you're renting or you're the owner of a condominium, you need to select the level of personal property coverage you desire. You can estimate this figure by totaling up the cost of replacing all your personal items.

You need to have a good grasp of what you own. Take an inventory of all your personal property, even if you don't need to total its value. The best way to do so is to take pictures or make a video. Be sure to take an inventory again every year or two or after you make some larger purchases. Also consider keeping receipts for the bigger-ticket items you buy for documentation purposes. No matter how you document your belongings, don't forget to keep the documentation somewhere besides your home — otherwise, it could be destroyed along with the rest of your house in a fire or other disaster.

I generally don't recommend paying for a *rider* for extra coverage (a rider is add-on coverage that specifically covers particular items not covered in your standard policy) unless you have items of significant value (such as artwork, jewelry, and so on).

Liability insurance

We live in a litigious society, so even though you may rightfully say the odds of someone suing you over an incident at your home are low, there's still a risk. *Liability insurance* protects you against legal claims due to an injury that occurs on your property. Get enough liability insurance to cover one to two times your financial assets.

As a renter, it's potentially useful to have liability protection. So in addition to insuring your personal property, another useful feature with renters insurance is liability coverage.

Natural disaster protection

A deficiency of homeowners insurance is that it generally doesn't cover damage to your home and personal property caused by earthquakes and floods. To cover such situations, you need to buy separate natural disaster protection coverage. For example, if your insurer estimates it would cost $200,000 to rebuild your home, you can buy a flood insurance policy through the Federal Emergency Management Agency (FEMA) that provides $200,000 of building coverage and $80,000 of contents coverage for about $368 annually if you live in a low-risk area. If you're a renter, simply get the $80,000 contents-only coverage for $208 per year.

Inquire with your current insurer or the insurers you shop among (such as those I recommend later in this chapter). If the cost of flood or earthquake insurance seems expensive, compare that expense to the costs you'd likely incur should your home and personal property be a total loss.

Shopping for homeowners insurance

To get the best homeowners insurance for the least cost, you can be proactive. Try these money-saving strategies:

- ✔ **Take a high deductible.** Because the objective of homeowners insurance is to protect against large losses, not small ones, take the highest deductible with which you're comfortable. Take into consideration how large an emergency reserve you have and the stability of your employment income.

- ✔ **Ask about special discounts.** If your property has a security system or you have other policies with the same insurer, you may qualify for a lower rate.

- ✔ **Improve your credit score.** Many insurers use your credit score (see Chapter 6) as a factor in setting some of your insurance rates. They do this because their studies have shown that folks who have higher credit scores tend to have fewer insurance claims.

- ✔ **Shop around.** Each insurance company prices its homeowners and renters policies based on its own criteria. So the lowest-cost company for your friend's property may not be the lowest-cost company for you. You have to shop around at several companies to find the best rates. Here's a list of companies that usually have lower-cost policies and do a decent job with customer satisfaction and claims paying:

- **Amica:** This company isn't the cheapest but it boasts high customer service ratings. Call Amica at 800-242-6422 or visit its Web site at www.amica.com.

- **Erie Insurance:** This firm operates mainly in the Midwest and Mid-Atlantic region. Check your local phone directory for agents. Call 800-458-0811 for a referral to a local agent or visit the company's Web site at www.erieinsurance.com.

- **GEICO:** You can contact this company by calling 888-530-5141 or by visiting its Web site at www.geico.com.

- **Liberty Mutual:** Check your local phone directory for agents, call 800-837-5254, or visit the company's Web site at www.libertymutual.com.

- **Nationwide Mutual:** Check your local phone directory for agents, call 877-669-6877, or visit the company's Web site at www.nationwide.com.

- **State Farm:** Check your local phone directory for agents or visit the company's Web site at www.statefarm.com.

- **USAA:** This company offers insurance to members of the military and their families. Call the company at 800-531-8722 or visit its Web site at www.usaa.com to see whether you qualify.

If you're interested in more information specific to your state, you may benefit from the information that your state insurance department collects regarding insurers' prices and complaints (not all states do this, however). Look up your state's department of insurance phone number in the government section of your local phone directory, or visit the National Association of Insurance Commissioners Web site at www.naic.org/state_web_map.htm to find links to each state's department of insurance site.

Driving safely

More than 30,000 people die annually in accidents on America's roads. Although this number has declined over the decades, it's still sad and tragically high, especially when you consider that many of these deaths are preventable. Here's what you can do to be on the good side of those statistics:

✓ **Drive a safe car.** Don't make the mistake of assuming that driving a safe vehicle requires buying a $50,000 high-end car. You don't need to spend buckets of money to get a car with desirable safety features. For a list of the safest cars, along with links for more information, visit my Web site: www.erictyson.com.

✓ **Drive safely.** Wear your seat belt! A U.S. Department of Transportation study found that 60 percent of auto passengers who were killed were not wearing their seat belts. Stay within the speed limit and don't drive while you're intoxicated or tired. And don't try to talk or text on your cellphone or any other communication device while driving. Use hands-free devices and minimize conversations while on the road.

✓ **Stay off the roads during the most dangerous times.** Extensive driving in the very late night/early morning hours and on major holidays (New Year's Eve, Independence Day, and so on) is asking for trouble given the preponderance of drunk drivers on the road. Also, be thoughtful about going on the road when the weather creates hazardous driving conditions.

Insuring Your Car

Although cars can be money pits, most people need them to get around. Cars are popular for good reason. You can transport yourself when and where you want in a car.

That said, if you choose to own a car, you can take important steps to minimize the car's costs. You need insurance but you don't need to waste money on it. This section explains exactly what you need.

Liability protection

Because of the inevitable accidents that happen with cars, auto insurance provides *liability protection* for injury caused to people and property. In fact, most states require this coverage by law. Liability protection comes in a couple of different forms:

- ✔ **Bodily injury liability:** This type covers injury to people. You should have sufficient bodily injury liability insurance to ideally cover at least twice the value of your assets.

  If you have little in the way of assets, know that your future earnings may be garnished in a lawsuit.

- ✔ **Property damage liability:** This type covers the property, which includes other people's cars. The level of property damage liability coverage in an auto policy is generally set based on the amount of bodily injury liability protection. Coverage of $50,000 is a good minimum to start with.

- ✔ **Uninsured or underinsured liability:** Auto policies also allow you to buy liability coverage for other motorists you may have an accident with who lack coverage or whose liability protection is minimal. This uninsured or underinsured motorist liability coverage allows you to collect for lost wages, medical expenses, and pain and suffering incurred in the accident.

If you already have comprehensive health and long-term disability insurance, uninsured or underinsured motorist liability coverage isn't really necessary. Just be aware that if you skip this coverage, you can't sue for general pain and suffering or insure passengers in your car who may lack adequate medical and disability coverage.

Collision and comprehensive

Collision coverage applies to claims arising from collisions of your car (and usually covers cars you rent as well). *Comprehensive coverage* is for claims for damage not caused by collision. For example, comprehensive coverage would cover damage done by someone breaking into your car.

Both collision and comprehensive coverage have their own deductible. For reduced auto insurance premiums, take the highest deductibles you can comfortably afford (I suggest at least $500 and ideally $1,000).

As your car ages and declines in value, you can eventually eliminate your comprehensive and collision coverage. Remember that insurers won't pay you more than your car's book value, regardless of what it costs to repair or replace it.

Riders you should bypass

You can add various optional coverages, known as *riders,* which appear to be inexpensive but really aren't when you compare the cost against the small amount of protection they provide. Here are common ones that auto insurers and agents pitch and that I would generally bypass:

- **Roadside assistance and towing:** These provisions provide coverage if your car breaks down. You may already have this protection if you belong to an auto club like AAA.

- **Rental car reimbursement:** This rider provides for a limited coverage amount for a rental car should your car be stolen or damaged and not drivable.

- **Riders that waive the deductible under certain circumstances:** The point of the deductible is to reduce your policy cost and eliminate the hassle of filing small claims.

- **Medical payments coverage:** This coverage typically pays a few thousand dollars for medical expenses. If you and your passengers carry major medical insurance coverage, this rider isn't really necessary. Besides, a few thousand dollars of medical coverage doesn't protect you against catastrophic expenses.

Getting a good buy

In the previous sections, I explain what you do and don't need on your auto insurance policy. Here are some additional ways to get the most for your money:

- **Consider insurance costs before buying your (next) car.** The cost of insuring a car should factor into your decision of which car you buy, because the insurance costs represent a major operating expense. Call insurers and ask for insurance price quotes for the different models you're considering before you buy.

✔ **Ask for special discounts.** A security alarm, antilock brakes, or other policies or cars insured with the same insurer may qualify your car for lower rates. And make sure that you're given appropriate "good driver" discounts if you've been accident- and ticket-free in recent years.

✔ **Shop among the best companies.** Use the insurers list I provide in the "Shopping for homeowners insurance" section earlier in this chapter to obtain quotes for auto insurance. In addition, also try Progressive (800-776-4737; www.progressive.com).

Umbrellas aren't just for bad weather

A good problem is having enough assets that you need additional liability protection beyond what's economical and available to buy on a home and auto policy. Enter *excess liability insurance* (also known as *umbrella* insurance), which is additional liability insurance that's added on top of the liability protection on your home and car(s).

Expect to pay $200+ annually for $1 million of coverage. Each year, thousands of people suffer lawsuits of more than $1 million related to their cars and homes.

So how do you decide how much you need if you have a lot of assets? You should have at least enough liability insurance to protect your assets, and preferably enough to cover twice the value of those assets.

Part V

Your Information Diet

"You may want to talk to Phil. He's one of our more aggressive financial planners."

In this part . . .

I discuss the vitally important topic of evaluating the quality and usefulness of money information and advice that you come across in the media or that you obtain by hiring someone. If you're hungry for financial information and advice, you're far more likely to gorge yourself and be overwhelmed than you are to end up malnourished! So I explain how to distinguish the best from the rest when you seek out information online, in print, and on radio and television. I also detail when it may make sense to hire help and how to go about doing so in a way that protects your interests and your wallet.

Chapter 16

Using Media Resources

● ●

● ●

*T*echnology and the Internet have rapidly changed the way people tap the vast and increasing amount of financial information and advice. Television, radio, magazines, and newspapers continue to attract plenty of eyeballs and listeners, of course, but those media have had to adapt and will continue to evolve because of the pressures of competition.

When I was a teenager and first took notice of the financial world, I was captivated, and so I observed, read, and learned all that I could about it. It's no surprise, then, that I landed in my current profession! What's amazing to me is how much things have changed and how much they haven't changed over the past three decades.

What has dramatically changed is where and how you can get financial advice and information. In the old days, you could consult lots of newspapers (especially the *Wall Street Journal*), some financial magazines, *Wall Street Week* on PBS television, and investment newsletters. Today, you can still refer to these sources for information (although fewer newspapers are around), and in addition, cable TV has seen a sharp increase in financial coverage on its many channels, and the Internet has tremendous numbers of financial Web sites and blogs.

What has stayed the same are the time-tested and common-sense principles of sound personal financial management and wise investments. Prognosticators who claim that they have a system for beating the system and the ability to produce fat profits are nothing new, and neither are the crooks who defraud folks out of their hard-earned money.

The challenge with all this financial information, advice, and predictions is to understand what's worth paying attention to and paying for and what you should ignore and perhaps even run away from! In this chapter, I discuss the various sources of financial advice and information and how to separate the best from the rest.

Going Online: The Wild West of Advice and Predictions

What has changed the most in recent years about financial advice and information is the enormous growth of the Internet. As with any medium, however, you need to remember the "buyer beware" mentality when looking for financial advice online. You can find lots of "free" stuff online, and therein lies one of the great dangers of the online world. I discuss this danger in this section, as well as how to make the most of what's useful on the Internet.

Eyeing the real cost of "free"

Whenever you read a personal finance article online that you don't have to pay for, ask yourself one simple question: How can the Web site purveyor afford to hire competent personal finance experts to write articles for the Web site? The answer for many sites is that they hope to make money from advertising. Their desire to make income from advertisers inevitably causes problems for you, dear reader, because it means that the Web site owner has to be careful to offer content that first and foremost is attractive for advertisers. As a result, Web sites may shy away from valid criticisms of various financial products, services, and firms. So what you may consider to be "free" content may actually have a hefty cost to you if it offers faulty advice that causes you future headaches and pain.

In the worst cases — and unfortunately, this is becoming increasingly common — companies pay Web sites to post flattering reviews of their products and services. Print publications generally have a tradition of disclosing when an article is paid advertising (known as an *advertorial*), but in the Wild West online, many sites fail to make this important disclosure. I'm not saying that disclosure makes advertorial content okay — but a failure to disclose makes an already bad situation even worse.

Also beware of links to recommended product and service providers to do business with. More often than not, the referring Web site gets paid an affiliate fee, sometimes amounting to 30, 40, or even 50+ percent of the product price. Look for sites that post policies against receiving such referral fees from companies whose products and services they recommend. (As an example, see the disclosure I use on my site, www.erictyson.com.)

Being aware online

If you want to best manage your personal finances and find out more, remember that the old expression "you get what you pay for" contains a grain of truth. Free information on the Internet, especially information provided by companies in the financial-services industry, is largely self-serving.

You can run into many pitfalls if you rely only on the Web for financial advice. Keep the following warnings in mind:

- ✔ **Beware of the short-term focus and addictive nature encouraged by many Web sites.** Many financial Web sites provide real-time stock quotes as a hook to a site that's cluttered with advertising. My experience in working with individual investors is that the more short term they think, the worse they do. And checking your portfolio during the trading day certainly promotes short-term thinking. Another way that sites create an addictive environment for you to return to multiple times daily is to constantly provide news and other rapidly changing content.

- ✔ **Beware of tips offered around the electronic water cooler — message boards.** As in the real world, chatting with strangers and exchanging ideas is sometimes fine. However, if you don't know the identity and competence of message-board posters or chat-room participants, why would you follow their financial advice or stock tips? Message boards are rife with day traders spreading exaggerations and lies in order to boost stock prices by a small amount and profit on a quick sale. Getting ideas from various sources is okay, but always verify the info with reliable sources. Educate yourself and do your homework before making personal financial decisions.

✔ **Stay away from the financial-planning advice offered by financial-services companies that are out to sell you something.** Such companies can't take the necessary objective, holistic view required to render useful advice.

Using the Web for gathering information

If you're looking for quality material written by unbiased experts or writers, finding it on the Web may seem like searching for the proverbial needle in the haystack, because much of what's online is biased and uninformed. Although I suggest you refer to proven professionals off-line, you can still use the Web in your personal financial research.

The following are some important financial tasks you can use the Internet for when gathering information, along with a short list of Web sites I recommend:

✔ **Planning for retirement:** Good retirement-planning online tools can help you plan for retirement by crunching the numbers for you. They can teach you how, for example, changes in your investment returns, the rate of inflation, or your savings rate can affect when and in what style you can retire. T. Rowe Price's Web site (www. troweprice.com) has several tools that can help you determine where you stand in terms of reaching a given retirement goal. Vanguard's Web site (www.vanguard. com) can help with figuring savings goals to reach retirement goals, as well as with managing your budget and assets in retirement.

✔ **Researching and trading investments:** You can choose from among many sites for dealing with your investments. The Securities and Exchange Commission (SEC) allows unlimited, free access to its documents at www. sec.gov. All public corporations, as well as mutual funds, file their reports with the agency. Be aware, however, that navigating this site takes patience. If you do your investing homework, trading securities online may save you money and perhaps some time. Online brokers such as E*TRADE Financial (800-387-2331; www.etrade.com) and Scottrade (800-619-7283; www.scottrade.com) have set a new, lower-cost standard. The major mutual fund companies, such as T. Rowe Price and Vanguard, also offer competitive online services.

Keeping an eye open for the agenda of expense tracking sites

Plenty of folks have trouble saving money and reducing their spending. Thus, it's no surprise that in the increasingly crowded universe of free Web sites, plenty of sites are devoted to supposedly helping you reduce your spending. These include Geezeo, Mint, Wesabe, and Yodlee.

I've reviewed these sites and have mixed-to-negative feelings about them. The biggest problem I have with these sites is that they're loaded with advertising and/or have affiliate relationships with companies (meaning that the site gets paid if you click on a link to one of its recommended service providers and buy what the provider is selling).

This arrangement, of course, creates an enormous conflict of interest and thoroughly taints any recommendation made by these sites that profit from affiliate referrals. For starters, they have no incentive or reason to recommend companies that don't pay them an affiliate fee. And there's little, if any, screening of companies for quality service levels that are important to you as a consumer.

Also, be forewarned that after registering you as a site user, the first thing most of these sites want you to do is connect directly to your financial institutions (banks, brokerages, investment companies, and so on) and download your investment account and spending data. Yes, you should have security concerns, but those pale in comparison to privacy concerns and concerns about the endless pitching to you of products and services.

Another problem I have with these Web sites is the incredibly simplistic calculators that they use. One site that purports to help with retirement planning doesn't allow users to choose a retirement age younger than 62 and has no provisions for part-time work. When this site asks about your assets, it makes no distinction between equity in your home and financial assets (stocks, bonds, mutual funds, and so on).

Finally, if you encounter a problem when using these sites, they generally offer no phone support, so you're relegated to ping-ponging e-mails in the hopes of getting your questions answered.

✔ **Buying life insurance:** If loved ones are financially dependent on you, you probably know that you need some life insurance. The best way to shop for term life insurance online is through one of the quotation services that I discuss in Chapter 14. At each of these sites, you fill in your date of birth, whether you smoke, how much coverage you'd like, and for how long you'd like to lock in the initial premium. When you're done filling in this information, you're provided with a list of low-cost quotes from highly rated insurance companies.

Some of the best Web sites allow you to more efficiently access information that may help you make important investing decisions. However, this doesn't mean that your computer allows you to compete at the same level as professional money managers. No, the playing field isn't level. The best pros in money management work at their craft full time and have far more expertise and experience than the rest of us. Some nonprofessionals have been fooled into believing that investing online makes them better investors. My experience has been that people who spend time online every day dealing with investments tend to react more to short-term events and have a harder time keeping the bigger picture and their long-term goals and needs in focus.

Getting Financial Perspectives and Advice from the Media

I'm well acquainted with the media. I used to write a regular financial advice column for the Sunday *San Francisco Chronicle,* and I continue to write a syndicated newspaper column (so long as some newspapers are still in existence!) and write regularly for my own Web site (www.erictyson.com). I've done thousands of interviews in various mediums, including radio, television, and print (magazines, newspapers, and many Web sites).

As with any profession, I've seen a range of expertise among the media people I've worked with. Here are some important things for you to keep in mind as a consumer of the media's personal finance coverage and coverage in general:

✔ **Remember that most reporters have little — and in some cases no — expertise regarding personal finance.** The best reporters are careful to write only about topics they have sufficient knowledge to tackle or topics for which they're willing and able to interview plenty of experts. Numerous personal finance articles and media pieces have errors and poorly reasoned premises, so beware and be educated in order to separate the best from the rest.

✔ **Be aware that the quest for ratings leads to hype.** Some news producers, in their quest for ratings and advertising dollars, try to be alarming to keep you tuned in and coming back for their "breaking news" updates. The more you watch, the more unnerved you get over short-term — especially negative — events. This can cause paralysis and unnecessary trading.

✔ **Reduce your exposure to advertising and the messages to spend, spend, and spend.** Coverage of movie stars and other celebrities implicitly and explicitly conveys that your worth as a person is related to your physical appearance (including the quality of clothing and jewelry you wear) and your material possessions — cars, homes, electronics, and other gadgets. Please don't buy into that false message.

✔ **Beware the catering to short attention spans.** Producers and network executives believe that if their content goes into too much detail, viewers and listeners will change the channel or turn the page. Many articles include more graphics and pictures than words to keep the reader's interest. Incomplete analysis can cause you to make poorly informed decisions.

✔ **Ignore the endless pundits who are interviewed for their predictions about the stock market, interest rates, and anything else that moves in the financial markets.** Prognosticating pundits keep many people tuned in because their advice is constantly changing (and is therefore entertaining and anxiety producing), and they lead investors to believe that investments can be maneuvered in advance to outfox future financial market moves. Remember: No one has a working crystal ball.

So should you ignore and shun all the media's personal finance coverage? Of course not — you simply need to distinguish between good and not-so-good financial information and advice. Here's how:

- ✔ **Pay attention to reporters' names and their strengths and weaknesses as you read articles.** As you read a given publication over time, you should begin to make note of the different writers. Get to know who the better writers are so you can spend your limited free time reading the best.

- ✔ **Review older articles and shows.** Although doing so may seem silly and pointless, it can actually be enlightening. By reviewing a number of past issues or shows in one sitting, you can begin to get a flavor for a publication's style, priorities, and philosophies (and you can also see how its past predictions turned out).

- ✔ **Look for solid information and perspective.** Headlines reveal a lot about how a columnist and publication perceive their roles. Sensationalist stories such as "The Next Meltdown Is Coming in 2012" and "These 13 'Tipping Points' Have Us on the Edge of a Depression" are playing into people's fears. Look for articles that seek to educate rather than make short-term predictions and create anxiety.

- ✔ **Keep your big-picture issues in mind.** Have you gotten your overall personal financial plan set? That's an important consideration when contemplating any specific financial advice you may hear or read.

- ✔ **Read the best books for a crash course on a given financial topic.** Good books can go into depth on a topic in a way that simply isn't possible with other resources. Good books also aren't cluttered with advertising and the conflicts inherent therein. (The worst ones are nothing more than infomercials to send you overpriced seminars, audiotapes, and so on.) For an updated list of my favorites, see my Web site at www.erictyson.com.

Chapter 17

Professionals You Hire

· ·

In This Chapter

▶ Working with financial advisors

▶ Getting tax help

▶ Navigating real estate deals

· ·

*O*ne of the benefits of living in a country with a relatively high standard of living is that many service providers are available for hire. Professionals can help with an array of services, but at a cost, and they aren't for everyone. When you're young and have a limited income, you probably can't afford to hire a fleet of financial, tax, legal, and other advisors.

Or perhaps you choose not to hire an army of professional advisors because you enjoy doing certain tasks yourself or you simply aren't comfortable delegating a task to someone you hire. Doing certain tasks yourself helps you broaden and enrich your hands-on knowledge, which can pay off down the road.

Whether or not you choose to hire a professional, having a firm understanding of a professional's role can help you make a wise choice. In this chapter, I discuss making the decision to hire help and the common advisors you may consider hiring. For each of these professionals, I offer tips on finding competent and ethical advice at a reasonable price.

Considering Financial Advisors

I worked for more than a decade as an hourly based financial advisor. Now as a financial counselor, I've fielded many questions from readers about their ups and downs with financial advisors. The main question you have to ask yourself is whether you even want to use a financial advisor. The following sections help you answer that question, locate quality professionals, and figure out what to ask before you hire.

Preparing to hire a financial advisor

I firmly believe that you're your own best financial advisor. However, some people don't want to make financial decisions without getting assistance. Perhaps you're busy or you simply can't stand making money decisions. And if you shy away from numbers, a good planner can help you.

Because I hear from many readers about problems with hiring incompetent and unethical financial advisors, before you hire a financial advisor, you need to understand the following points:

✔ **Educate yourself.** You need to know enough about the topic so that you can at least tell whether the person knows his stuff. For starters, how can you possibly hope to evaluate the expertise of someone you may hire if you're not at least modestly educated on the topic yourself? Most personal financial decisions aren't that complex, so the more you know, the more responsibility you can take for making the best decisions for your situation.

✔ **Understand how compensation creates conflicts of interest.** When financial consultants/advisors sell products that earn them sales commissions (for example, investments, insurance, and so on), that arrangement can easily bias their recommendations. Financial planners who perform ongoing money management have a conflict of interest as well, because anything that takes away money for them to manage (for example, paying down debt, buying a home or other real estate, and so on) is of less interest to them.

✔ **Ask questions before hiring an advisor.** Take referrals as leads to check on. Never take a referral from anyone as gospel. Do your homework before hiring any advisor.

A quality financial planner doesn't come cheaply, so make sure that you want and need to hire an advisor before searching for a competent one. If you have a specific tax or legal matter, you may be better off hiring a good professional who specializes in that specific field rather than hiring a financial planner.

Recognize that you have a lot at stake when you hire a financial advisor. You're placing a lot of trust in his recommendations. The more you know, the better the advisor you end up working with, and the fewer services you need to buy.

Finding good financial advisors

So where and how can you find the best financial advisors? Here are three places to start searching:

- ✔ **The American Institute of Certified Public Accountants Personal Financial Specialists:** The AICPA (888-999-9256; `http://apps.aicpa.org/credentialsrefweb/PFSCredentialSearchPage.aspx`) is a professional association of CPAs. The organization compiles a list of its members who have completed its Personal Financial Specialist (PFS) program, many of whom provide financial advice on a fee basis. Competent CPAs understand the tax consequences of different choices, which are important components of any financial plan. On the other hand, keeping current in two broad fields can be hard for some professionals.

- ✔ **The National Association of Personal Financial Advisors:** The NAPFA (800-366-2732; `www.napfa.org`) consists of fee-only planners. Its members aren't supposed to earn commissions from products they sell or recommend. However, most planners in this association earn their living by providing money-management services and charging a fee that's a percentage of assets under management. Most have minimums, which can put them out of reach for some people.

- ✔ **Personal referrals:** Getting a personal referral from a satisfied customer you trust is one of the best ways to find a good financial planner. Obtaining a referral from an accountant or attorney whose judgment you've tested can help as well. Remember, though, that regardless of who makes the referral, do your own investigation. Ask the planner the questions I list in the next section, "Interviewing advisors." Remember that the person who makes the recommendation is (probably) not a financial expert, and the person may simply be returning the favor of business referrals from the financial advisor.

Interviewing advisors

Take your time and fully interview any prospective advisor you may hire with the following important questions:

- ✔ **What percentage of your income comes from commissions, hourly client fees, and client money-management fees?** If you want objective and specific financial planning recommendations, give preference to advisors who derive their income from hourly fees. Many counselors and advisors call themselves *fee-based,* which usually means that they make their living managing money for a percentage. If you want a money manager, you can hire the best quite inexpensively through a mutual fund. If you have substantial assets, you can hire an established money manager.

Advisors who provide investment advice and manage at least $25 million must register with the U.S. Securities and Exchange Commission (SEC). You can find out whether the advisor is registered and whether he has a track record of problems by calling the SEC at 800-732-0330 or by visiting its Web site at www.adviserinfo.sec.gov. Otherwise, advisors generally must register with the state in which they make their principal place of business. They must file Form ADV, otherwise known as the *Uniform Application for Investment Adviser Registration.* You can ask the advisor to send you a copy of Form ADV, which includes such juicy details as a breakdown of where the advisor's income comes from, the advisor's relationships and affiliations with other companies, the advisor's education and employment history, and the advisor's fee schedule.

- ✔ **What work and educational experience qualify you to be a financial planner?** A planner should have experience in the business or financial services field and should also be good with numbers, speak in plain English, and have good interpersonal skills. Common designations of educational training among professional money managers are MBA (master of business administration) and CFA (chartered financial analyst). Some tax advisors who work on an hourly basis have the PFS (personal financial specialist) credential. The CFP (certified financial planning) degree is common among those focusing their practice on financial planning.

✔ **What is your hourly fee?** The rates for financial advisors range from as low as $75 per hour all the way up to several hundred dollars per hour. If you shop around, you can find fine planners who charge around $100 to $150 per hour. Focus on the total cost that you can expect to pay for the services you're seeking.

✔ **In addition to financial advisory services, what other services do you perform (such as tax or legal services)?** Tread carefully with someone who claims to be an expert beyond one area. The tax, legal, and financial fields are vast in and of themselves, and they're difficult for even the best and brightest advisor to cover simultaneously. An exception is the tax advisor/preparer who performs basic financial planning by the hour. Likewise, a good financial advisor should have a solid grounding in the basic tax and legal issues that relate to your personal finances. Large firms may have specialists available in different areas.

✔ **Do you carry professional liability insurance?** If the advisor doesn't have liability insurance, she has missed one of the fundamental concepts of planning: Insure against risk. After all, you want an advisor who carries protection in case she makes a major mistake for which she's liable.

✔ **Can you provide references from clients with needs similar to mine?** Interview others who've used the planner. Ask what the planner did for them, and find out what the advisor's strengths and weaknesses are. You can find out a bit about the planner's track record and style.

✔ **Will you provide specific strategies and product recommendations that I can implement if I choose?** This question is crucial because some advisors may indicate that you can hire them by the hour but provide only generic advice. Ideally, find an advisor who lets you choose whether you want to hire her to help implement her recommendations after she presents them. If you know that you're going to follow through on the advice and you can do so without further discussions and questions, don't hire the planner to help you implement her recommendations. On the other hand, if you hire the counselor because you lack the time, desire, and/or expertise to manage your financial life, building implementation into the planning work makes good sense.

Taming Your Taxes with Help

Taxes are likely one of your biggest expenses. No one enjoys paying so much in taxes, complying with seemingly endless tax rules and regulations, and completing federal- and state-mandated tax returns. So it should come as no surprise that an army of tax preparers and advisors is standing ready to help you.

Do you need to use a tax professional? Good tax preparers and advisors can save you money by identifying tax-reduction strategies you may overlook. And they may reduce the likelihood of your being audited, which can be triggered by mistakes. Tax advisors can be of greater use to folks whose financial lives have changed significantly (those who are starting a small business, for instance) and to people who are unwilling to learn tax strategies to reduce their tax burden.

Tax advisors and preparers come with varying backgrounds, training, and credentials. Here are the three main types, with some info that can help you determine which one is right for you:

- **Preparers:** The appeal of *preparers,* who generally are unlicensed, is that they're comparatively less costly (their rate works out to less than $100 per hour) than other tax professionals. Preparers make the most sense for folks who have relatively simple financial lives, who are budget-minded, and who dislike doing their own taxes.

- **Enrolled agents:** A person must pass IRS licensing requirements to be called an *enrolled agent* (EA), which enables the agent to represent you before the IRS. Continuing education is also required; EAs generally go through more training than preparers. EAs are best for people who have moderately complex returns and don't necessarily need complicated tax-planning advice throughout the year (although some EAs provide this service as well). You can find contact information for EAs in your area by calling the National Association of Enrolled Agents at 202-822-6232 or visiting its Web site at www.naea.org.

- **Certified public accountants:** CPAs go through significant training and examination before receiving the CPA credential. And to maintain the designation, CPAs also must complete continuing education classes annually. Most CPAs charge $100+ per hour. CPAs at larger firms and in high-cost-of-living areas tend to charge more. CPAs make the most sense for the self-employed and/or for folks who file lots of other schedules with their tax returns.

Working with Real Estate Agents

When you buy or sell a property such as a condominium, town home, or single family home, if you're like most people, you'll likely work with a real estate agent who's paid on commission. Although the best real estate agents can help you find a home that meets your needs, the commission arrangement can create conflicts of interest. Because agents get a percentage of your property's sales price, they want you to complete a deal quickly and at the highest price possible. When you're a seller, the agent's incentives can be good, but when you're a buyer, they can be in conflict with what's best for you.

Some buyer's agents say that they can better represent your interests as a property buyer and will sign a contract with you to represent you as a buyer's agent. However, agents working as buyer's brokers to represent you still have conflicts of interest in that they get paid only when you buy and earn a commission as a percentage of the purchase price.

To find a good real estate agent, begin by interviewing at least three agents. Ask the agents for references from at least three clients they worked with in the past six months in the geographical area in which you're looking. Look for agents with the following traits:

- ✔ **Local market knowledge:** Investigating communities, school systems, neighborhoods, and financing options can be a huge undertaking. Good agents can help you tap into various information sources as well as share their contacts with you.

- ✔ **Full time and experienced:** Ask how many years the agent has been working full time. The best agents work at their profession full time so that they can stay on top of everything. Many of the best agents come into the field from other occupations, such as business or teaching. Some sales, marketing, negotiation, and communication skills can certainly be picked up in other fields, but experience in buying and selling real estate does count.

✔ **Honesty and patience:** A real estate purchase or sale is typically a large-dollar transaction from the perspective of your overall personal finances. So you need an agent who always answers your questions truthfully and who always goes out of his way to disclose anything that could affect properties you're considering. You also need a patient agent who's willing to allow you the necessary time to get educated and make your best decision.

✔ **Negotiation and interpersonal skills:** Putting a deal together involves lots of negotiation. Ask the agent's references how well the agent negotiated for them. Also, your agent needs to represent your interests and get along with other agents, property sellers, inspectors, mortgage lenders, and so on.

✔ **High-quality standards:** Sloppy work can lead to big legal or logistical problems down the road. If an agent neglects to recommend thorough and complete inspections, for example, you may be stuck with undiscovered problems after the deal.

Part VI
The Part of Tens

The 5th Wave   By Rich Tennant

"I think I have a pretty good savings plan. I plan to save 15 percent on a Rolex watch this weekend."

In this part . . .

You find some bite-size and fun chapters on ten ways to save money on a car and ten things more important than your money. Why "tens"? Why not?

Chapter 18

Ten Ways to Save on a Car

▶ Understanding the smart ways to buy a car

▶ Comparing different cars' costs

▶ Servicing, insuring, and taking tax deductions for your car

1 remember my first car and appreciate the flexibility and joy that having that car provided me. My first car was a generously sized Ford LTD that was a hand-me-down. No longer able to drive, my elderly grandfather had given the car to my parents. After a couple years of additional use, my folks then passed the car along to me when I got my first job and was working in Boston. I didn't have much free time or need to use the car during the workweek but I was grateful to have it for weekend trips.

In some respects, it was an ideal first car because it was solid and reliable but not overly valuable. It probably didn't get great gas mileage, but I appreciated its safety when a car (a compact) rear-ended my car and barely left a scratch (although the front end of the bad driver's car was totaled).

In this chapter, I highlight some tips and strategies for making the most of your car-driving experiences and doing so in a financially prudent fashion. For more information on other transportation options to help you save money, check out Chapter 4.

Don't Buy a Car in the First Place

My first experience owning a car taught me an important lesson: Car ownership is costly. As a result, I suggest that if you don't need a car, then don't buy one, particularly if you live in a city with reliable public transportation. Use the subway or bus and save your money. As with renting a home or apartment instead of buying and owning one, sometimes in your life you may be able to do without your own car, and other times you'll feel that having a car is 100 percent necessary. Enjoy the times when you can do without a car because you may save a good deal of money and hassle.

Owning a car requires multiple expenses that can really drain your wallet. In addition to insurance and gas, in my experience with my first car, I faced a seemingly never-ending list of maintenance and repairs, and that list only grew worse the longer I had the car. And having a car in a big city can be a hassle — I had to pay parking tickets from parking my car on the Boston streets and had to deal with not always being available to move the car on designated street-sweeping days. Add the expense of having to pay out of pocket for damages likely caused by a city snowplow that didn't own up to the accident.

When I moved from Boston and over the subsequent decade, many of the years I chose not to own a car. I was able to do this because I lived either in a city with decent public transit options or in the suburbs close to everything I needed and could manage well with a bike (in a nice year-round climate!). During those years when I didn't have a car, I would rent one on occasion, and that worked out well and was far more economical than owning my own car.

Pay Cash: Shun Leasing and Borrowing

When you do decide to get your own car, do your best to save in advance and pay for the car with your cash savings. For many folks starting out, doing so means setting their sights on a good-quality used car.

Taking out a loan to buy a car or leasing a car are generally much-more expensive ways to get a car because of the interest you pay (in the case of a loan) or the higher rates (in the case of leasing). Car dealers who are in the business of leasing or originating car loans will, of course, have a different agenda and push these methods because they profit from them. Don't be fooled by zero percent interest loans, either — dealers will sock you with a higher car price to make up for such low-cost financing.

Consider Total Costs

When you compare makes and models of cars, be sure to consider more than the sticker price. Among other cost considerations are fuel, maintenance, repairs, insurance, and how rapidly the car depreciates in value.

Among the best independent sources that I've found for such information are www.edmunds.com and www.intellichoice.com.

Compare New with Used

Because a new car depreciates most rapidly in value in the first couple of years, buying a car that's at least a year or two old usually provides you with a better value for your money than buying a new car.

Don't assume, however, that buying a used car is always a better value. For example, during a severe recession such as the one the United States experienced in the late 2000s, new cars made comparatively better sense than many used cars. The reason for this was a matter of simple economics and supply and demand. More people opted for buying a used car. Fewer folks put theirs on the market, holding off on buying a new one until the economy got better. These two forces squeezed supply and increased prices. At the same time, fewer consumers were buying new cars, forcing dealers to slash prices.

Understand a Car's Real Value before Negotiating

After you home in on what make and model of car you want, make sure that you arm yourself with the essential information as you shop around. For new cars, you should know (and can easily find out) what the dealer's cost is for each vehicle. You can find this information at *Consumer Reports* as well as the sources I mention in the next paragraph.

For used cars, a number of sources can assist you with quickly valuing a vehicle based on its condition, features, and mileage. Among the best sources for used car valuation information are Kelly Blue Book and Edmunds.

Take Care of Your Car

Besides the obvious financial benefit from staying on top of your car's servicing requirements (getting your oil changed regularly, rotating and properly inflating your tires, and so on), you also reap safety benefits as well. That's why you should be proactive about your car's maintenance. (See Chapter 15 for more ideas.)

Of course, not everyone is. I was astonished to see a car with nearly completely bald tires at the local garage that services my car. I subsequently learned that the woman refused to replace her tires because she "couldn't afford" to do so. (Never mind that she was driving a more costly car than I was!) Clearly, she could afford to do so, but for whatever odd reason (more than likely ignorance about the danger), she wasn't spending her money on new tires. By driving on such old tires, she was causing other problems to her car and, of course, risking a serious accident, which would really lead to a large bill and possible injury (or worse) to her and others.

Explore Your Servicing Options

Finding a good auto mechanic — someone who's competent and honest — is no small feat! You're not likely an expert in the various components and operating systems of your car, so you're largely at the mercy of the mechanic telling you that you supposedly need to have something addressed on your car.

The primary advantage of taking your car to an authorized dealer (such as taking your Honda to a Honda dealer) is that the dealer has the proper equipment and technology to test and service your car. The downside to dealers is that they may have higher rates and may push doing packages of work at major mileage milestones (for example, 30,000 miles, 60,000 miles, and so on) that don't really need to be done.

Numerous local garages can do the work, and the primary advantage with those can be convenience (choosing one near your home or office) and possibly lower rates. However, an unscrupulous mechanic may push doing work that doesn't need to be done, and you also need to be on the lookout for competence issues, as an independent mechanic may not be able to service the full range of problems on your car's make and model.

Drive Safely

Driving faster than 60 miles per hour, accelerating too fast, and having to jam on the breaks wastes gas and adds to the wear and tear on your car over time (and therefore is costly). And what about the people traveling with you? Driving is probably the most dangerous thing you do on a regular basis, so it's not just about your money but the health and safety of you, your friends, and your family who take trips in your car. See Chapter 15 for details on safe driving and safe cars.

Take a Lean and Mean Insurance Policy

Most states mandate minimum levels of auto insurance. In my experience as a financial counselor reviewing folks' insurance policies, including their auto insurance, people often have the wrong types of coverage — missing things they really need while wasting money on other things they don't need. Be sure to review my auto insurance recommendations in Chapter 15.

Track Tax-Deductible Auto Expenses

You may be able to deduct certain auto expenses related to the use of your car for your job, especially if you're self-employed. Be aware, however, that your expenses for commuting in your car between your home and office aren't deductible.

You can deduct your out-of-pocket expenses (such as gas and oil) that are directly related to the use of your car in charitable work. You can't deduct anything like general repair or maintenance expenses, tires, insurance, depreciation, and so on. If you don't want to track and deduct your actual expenses, the IRS allows you to use a standard rate per mile to figure your contribution. You can deduct actual expenses for parking fees and tolls. If you must travel away from home to perform a real and substantial service, such as attending a convention for a qualified charitable organization, you can claim a deduction for your unreimbursed travel and transportation expenses, including meals and lodging. Such deductions are only allowed if your travel involves no significant amount of personal pleasure.

Chapter 19

Ten Things to Value More Than Your Money

In This Chapter

▶ Keeping the bigger picture in mind

▶ Minding your neighbors and those in need

*T*hroughout this book, I provide information and advice that can help you make the most of your money. Whether you've stuck with me since Chapter 1 or simply skimmed a few chapters, you probably know that I take a holistic approach to money decisions.

Although I hope my financial advice serves you well, I also want to be sure that you remember the many things in life that are far more important than the girth of your investment portfolio or the size of your latest paycheck. I hope this chapter of ten things more valuable than money makes a small contribution to keeping you on the best overall path.

Investing in Your Health

People neglect their health for different reasons. In some cases, as with money management, people simply don't know the keys to good personal health. Getting too caught up in one's career and working endless hours also often lead to neglect of one's health.

Plenty of people suffer from ongoing conditions that damage their body and make them feel worse than need be. Stress, poor diet, lack of exercise, problematic relationships — all these bad habits can harm your health. You only get one body — take care of it and treat it with the respect it deserves!

Making and Keeping Friends

So many items in this consumer-oriented society are disposable, and unfortunately, friends too often fall into that category. These days, it seems like friends aren't really friends as much as they are acquaintances who can further people's careers, and after that function has passed, they're cast aside.

Ask yourself who your true friends are. Do you have friends you can turn to in a time of need who can really listen and be there for you? Take the time to invest in your friendships, both old and new.

Appreciating What You Have

In my work as a financial counselor and writer, I've had the opportunity to interact with many people from all walks of life. Rich or poor, invariably people focus on what they don't have instead of appreciating the material and nonmaterial things they do have.

Make a list of at least ten things that you appreciate. Periodically (weekly or monthly) make another list. This exercise helps you dwell on what you have instead of dwelling on what you don't.

Minding Your Reputation

One of my professors once said, "It can take a lifetime to build a reputation but only moments to lose it." As people chase after more fame, power, money, and possessions, they often devalue and underinvest in relationships and commit illegal and immoral acts along the way. Your reputation is one of the most important things you have, so don't do anything to taint it.

Think of the people you most admire in your life. Although I'm sure that none of them is perfect, I bet each has a superior reputation in your eyes.

Continuing Education

Education is a lifelong process — it's not just about attending a pricey college and perhaps getting an advanced degree. You always have something to discover, whether it's related to your career or a new hobby. Look for opportunities to master new lessons each and every day. And who knows, maybe someday you'll gain an understanding of the meaning of life. The older people get, the more they have to reflect upon and benefit from.

Having Fun

In the quest to earn and save more, some people get caught up in society's money game that money becomes the purpose of their existence. They lose sight of what life is really about. Whether you call it an addiction or an obsession, having such a financial focus steers you from life's good things. I've known plenty of people who realize too late in life that sacrificing personal relationships and one's health isn't worth any amount of financial success.

Therapists' offices are filled with unhappy people who spend too much time and energy chasing elusive career goals and money. These same people come to me for financial counseling and worry about having enough money. When I tell them that they have "enough," the conversation usually turns to the personal things lacking in their life. Remember to keep your perspective and live each day to the fullest.

Putting Your Family First

Some employees rightfully fear that their boss may not be sympathetic to their family's needs, especially when those needs get in the way of getting the job done as efficiently as an impatient boss would like. Others put their company first because that's what peers do and because they don't want to rock the boat.

Your spouse, your parents, and your kids, of course, should come first. They're more important than your next promotion, so treat them that way. Balance is key; your actions speak louder than promises and words. Should your boss not respect or value the importance of family, then perhaps it's time to find a new boss.

Knowing Your Neighbors

Your neighbors can be sources of friendship, happiness, and comfort. I often see people caught up in their routine who neglect their neighbors. You live by these people and probably see them on a semiregular basis. Take the time to get to know them.

You may not want to get to know all your neighbors better, but give them a chance. Don't write them off because they aren't the same age, race, or occupation as you. Part of your coherence with greater society comes from where you live, and your neighbors are an important piece of that connection.

Volunteering and Donating

Although the United States has one of the world's highest per-capita incomes, by other, more important measures, the country has room for improvement. Society has some significant problems, such as a relatively high rate of poverty, gun violence, divorce, and suicide.

You can find plenty of causes worthy of your volunteer time or donations. Check out www.volunteermatch.org to discover volunteer opportunities. If you want to donate something as a thank-you to members of the military, visit www.militaryfamily.org. (Military folks can use this site to find out about a wide range of benefits.)

Caring for Kids

The children in society are tomorrow's future. You should care about children even if you don't have any. Why? Do you care about the quality of society? Do you have any concerns about crime? Do you care about the economy? What about your Social Security and Medicare benefits? All these issues depend to a large extent on the nation's children and what kind of teenagers and adults they someday become.

Investing in your children and other children is absolutely one of the best investments you can make. Understanding how to relate to and care for kids can help make you a better and more fulfilled person. (And I think that understanding kids can help you better understand what makes grown-ups tick, too!)

Index